NONE OF OUR
BUSINESS

DATE DUE

NONE OF OUR BUSINESS

Why Business Models Don't Work *in Schools*

CRYSTAL M. ENGLAND

HEINEMANN
PORTSMOUTH, NH

Heinemann
A division of Reed Elsevier Inc.
361 Hanover Street
Portsmouth, NH 03801–3912
www.heinemann.com

Offices and agents throughout the world

© 2003 by Crystal M. England

The author and publisher wish to thank those who have generously given permission to reprint borrowed material:

Excerpts from "Homeless Children" from *America Magazine,* November 13, 1999, are reprinted by permission of America Press. Copyright © 1999. All rights reserved (www.americamagazine.org).

Excerpts from "Companies Target Large States When the Stakes Are High" are reprinted by permission from *Education Week,* Vol. 20, Number 26, March 14, 2001.

Excerpts from "Bush Still Pushing Vouchers" (2/4/2002) are reprinted by permission of the Associated Press.

Excerpts from "School Choice: As Education Reform" by Dan Goldhaber are reprinted from *Phi Delta Kappan,* October, 1997, by permission of the author.

Library of Congress Cataloging-in-Publication Data
England, Crystal M.
    None of our business : why business models don't work in schools / author, Crystal M. England.
        p.   cm.
    Includes bibliographical references.
    ISBN 0-325-00444-7 (pbk. : alk. paper)
    1. Industry and education—United States.   2. Education—Aims and objectives—United States.   3. Education—Standards—United States.
    4. Education and state—United States.   I. Title.

    LC1085.2 .E3895 2003
    371.19′5—dc21   2002151784

Editor: Lois Bridges
Production service: bookworks
Production coordinator: Lynne Reed
Cover design: Jenny Jensen Greenleaf
Cover photograph: Library of Congress, Prints and Photographs Division, National Child Labor Committee Collection, NWDNS-102-LH-220.
Typesetter: TechBooks
Manufacturing: Steve Bernier

Printed in the United States of America on acid-free paper
07   06   05   04   03   DA   1   2   3   4   5

To Mom, Dad, and Alexander . . . for always believing

CONTENTS

INTRODUCTION

I was freezing. Temperature controlled. Dressed in sterile white from gloves to gown. I wore earplugs for my protection against the grind and the whir and the buzz of productivity in motion. And the evenly round pizza crusts went by me with military efficiency, even the droplets of sauce that fell did so in uniform repetition. At the rate of 7000 an hour, the production manager proudly told me. I was impressed by the clean efficiency, the measures taken to secure against contamination, the way the standards could be enforced time and again and again and again.

Another day. Another tour. But a very different type of plant. Noisy still, but the young workers were unprotected from the fray. Harried production managers with chalk dust on their hands were still trying to account for missing ingredients from the day before. The temperature was controlled by the sun and today the creativity centers were laden with the stench of sweat. The broken fan did little to stimulate air flow. Eyelids drooped and the supervisor watched in dismay as production rates declined. Workers slumped in their chairs, the straight rows of their seats the only indicator of orderliness that remained. Slowly the hands on the clock ticked until suddenly lights flickered and bells rang. And the doors opened with a modicum of efficiency. The products abandoned their desks and flooded the hallways. Laughing, talking, cursing, crying. Contaminants asserted their "right" to be present. Loudspeakers bleated directions and controls, thwarting communication. The product was tangled, in a chaos so typical that it had become status quo. At the rate of 700 an hour.

For some years now, advocates for public school reform, like Martin Gross, Myron Lieberman, and even President George W. Bush have been likening public schools to businesses. They pull their analogies out of their pockets and gaze at them fondly, tucking them carefully away and getting on with the business of rhetoric and impracticality, satisfied that at last they have told us what we needed to know. If only we in the trenches would use quality principles, sound marketing, and other basic tenets of big business to mold our product, perhaps American schools would not be trailing so far behind other nations of comparable socioeconomic status. The assertion has been that with more front-end management and an increasingly open market, that schools could indeed experience the success of a corporation. This book examines this assumption at its core and leaves the reader to decide . . . is education an art or an industry? Which matters more . . . product or process?

CHAPTER ONE

IT TAKES A VILLAGE TO RAISE
A CHILD

Educational institutions contend with many different "publics."
This chapter provides an overview of the expectations currently
placed on schools, compares those expectations to that of the
corporate structure, and provides the groundwork for the issues
covered in more depth in subsequent chapters of the book.

IT TAKES A VILLAGE...

Hillary Rodham Clinton brought this message to many homes.
We like to say it. It rolls off our tongues and gives us the warm
fuzzy feeling of security, that of a communal stake in the future
of our youth. But it is a false security, at best. How many times
has your car manufacturer called to ask your advice? What about
the producer of your dish detergent? Your personal computer?
What would you say if Duracell called to ask which production
line to run next Tuesday?

You might be able to hazard a guess. You might throw your
hands up in agitation. Or you may roll your eyes and wonder
why you are being asked something so far out of your realm
of expertise. Having never invented a safety belt, experimented
with the chemicals in dish detergent, or stepped foot inside a bat-
tery factory, you may feel ill equipped to handle questions that
so closely affect the outcome of a product. Your apprehension
would be reasonable. Common sense dictates that successful

companies hire the best and the brightest to aid in manufacturing quality goods. True, public opinion is important. But the development of a public trust is a far better indicator of long-term success.

How does an industry build trust? The most basic answer lies in a systematic approach to quality control. Extreme measures are taken to make certain that the raw goods put into a product meet standards. They are poked, prodded, weighed, measured, examined under microscopes, and blasted by extremes in temperature and light. And they are rejected, yanked out of line by a wide system of controls. Given to another market, perhaps. Recycled, maybe. Possibly simply tossed away. It doesn't matter. The important part to remember is that the flaws do not make it to the public eye, the public plate, or the public roads.

HERE A STUDENT, THERE A STUDENT...

Eighty-nine percent of adults have attended public schools. Of the remaining 11 percent, 80 percent attended a private school for reasons of religious education.[1] All comprise a body of contributing taxpayers in their community. All have ideas on what a school should be. The perceived ingredients of a learning environment are not complex. A plot of land, a brick building, teachers, students, chalk, textbooks, and stern-faced administrators round out the simple picture. The village that has the responsibility to raise the child has walked the halls of the plant. They have, at some point in their lives, talked to the workers, turned the pages of the tools, and beat the chalk from countless erasers against the vaguely eroded bricks. They feel secure in making production decisions, glad to hire a board of controls from among their ilk, and gladder still, to proffer advice while bemoaning the quality of the product. Even Socrates complained of the children in his generation, "Our youth now love luxury. They have bad manners, contempt for authority; they show disrespect for their elders and love chatter in place of exercise; they no longer rise when elders enter the room; they contradict their parents, chatter before company; gobble of their food and tyrannize their teachers."

Arguably, an informed public should be an asset. Those that truly understand what creates a quality product can be instrumental in the management of the outcome. In the kismet of educational design, the throng of village workers are informed, committed, and are *using the same standard to judge quality.* But this is not always the case. On any given day, the dysfunctional and the embittered wander the floors, and as the ashes fall from the acrid tips of their opinions, they snipe at the supervisors, hack at the budget, and embrace a "good enough" philosophy with regard to production. How many times have we heard, "Well, I didn't have a fancy computer and I turned out all right. It was good enough for me," or "We didn't have all those special education classes and we got by . . . it was good enough for us," or "My classroom was crowded but I survived . . . it was good enough for me." Remember those impressive standards in the pizza factory? The investors in the public realm make them impossible.

It was my second year as a school principal. I wanted to build trust. I had the eight district outcomes for all learners memorized and idolized. We were going to make a difference. We were going to ultimately graduate well-rounded, capable, open-minded individuals. Armed with this knowledge, I was ready for the phone call. It was from "anonymous," one of the many brave enough to share an opinion but not a name. She had received a field trip form about a local musical production that we were taking the students to see. Her question was direct, "Why are you taking the children to see a play?"

The hostility was evident in her voice but I was ready. My answer was succinct, "Well, one of our district outcomes is to help our students become artistic appreciators and this production not only enhances our curriculum, it helps move us toward that goal."

She said, "Yeah, right, wasting time for everyone. Didn't you go to a play last year? Why do you ever need to go to another one?" There was little more to say except "thank you for calling to share your concern" but had I waited, I am sure I would have heard that hallowed phrase, "I never went to a play...and it was good enough for me."

THE STANDARDS BANDWAGON

Improbability does not prevent action. *Standards* and *benchmarks* have replaced the words *goals* and *outcomes* in educational jargon. All states and schools have challenging and clear standards of achievement and accountability for all children, and effective strategies for reaching those standards.[2] National standards across content areas have been developed by companies such as McRel.[3] The rationale behind this movement is best expressed in the following, excerpted from the McRel Website <www.mcrel.org>:

> Amid growing concerns about the educational preparation of the nation's youth, President Bush and the nation's governors called an Education Summit in Charlottesville in September 1989. That summit concluded with the establishment of six broad goals for education that were to be reached by the year 2000. The goals and their rationale are published under the title *The National Education Goals Report: Building a Nation of* Learners (National Education Goals Panel [NEGP], 1991). Two of the goals (3 and 4) related specifically to academic achievement:
>
>> Goal 3: By the year 2000, American students will leave grades 4, 8, and 12 having demonstrated competency in challenging subject matter including English, mathematics, science, history, and geography; and every school in America will ensure that all students learn to use their minds well, so they may be prepared for responsible citizenship, further learning, and productive employment in our modern economy.
>>
>> Goal 4: By the year 2000, U.S. students will be first in the world in science and mathematics achievement.
>
> The goals were outlined in the State of the Union of 1990, a year which also saw Congress establish the National Education

4

Goals Panel (NEGP); the following year, Congress established the National Council on Education Standards and Testing (NCEST). Collectively, these two groups were charged with addressing unprecedented questions regarding American education such as, What is the subject matter to be addressed? What types of assessments should be used? What standards of performance should be set?

With the establishment of educational standards, bureaucrats everywhere breathed a collective sigh of relief. The greatest of educational reform movements was under way! Now there would be an articulated, quantifiable way to measure students, teachers, and subsequently an entire educational system. All of the necessities of a well-rounded education were available in print and all the teachers had to do was find a way to teach them.

I wish I could have taken Jason to their summit. Jason was a second grader when I met him. He sat in the third desk in the first row of my classroom for students with special needs. On a good day, he scribbled through his work with an odd system of dashes and dots that represented printing. On a bad day he pulled out his eyelashes and drew detailed pictures of nuclear substations on countless pieces of scrap paper. On most days, he did both. The first necessity of his well-rounded education was to help him have more good days. I looked but I didn't find that objective in the standards anywhere.

I can hear the political protest. Jason is the exception and not the rule. We have special laws and policies for Jason. For all others though, the standards provide a quantifiable means to measure learning. But how to measure if they were being taught? For policy makers, the answer seemed simple. It couldn't be enough to trust that the professionals were doing their job. After all, policy makers had walked the halls of the plant and seen inefficiency in motion too many times for that. The answer had to lie in testing. All across America, national testing companies seized the opportunity to work with state-level diagnosticians and design a test that would truly measure the standards inherent in the new and improved mandated curriculum. And since the curricular standards were mandated, it seemed only logical that the tests be mandated, too. Students everywhere in grades 4, 8,

10, and 12 became the heartbeat of the school. These were the examples of American education. Schools everywhere held their breath as they watched the efforts of their teachers melt down to a single indicator of success. And the politicians danced on the crest of the newest wave in reform.

Anyone in the field of education would be unprofessional and foolhardy to deny the importance of curricular goals. They would be inept if they did not espouse a curriculum that equipped all students across America to become productive world citizens with a sound base of knowledge. Standards in and of themselves are quality tools that should be available to all within a school that works with children. But let's return to the pizza plant and extend the analogy. Suppose that the corporation was judged only on the production of pizzas containing a certain number of prescribed ingredients. Each pizza that came off the line would be judged a success if it contained the cheese, sauce, and pepperoni that it was supposed to contain. Certainly, a great number of successful pizzas could be produced, but if no one ever thought to perform other critical tasks, such as taste testing, market analysis by geographic location, or the current supply and demands of the consumer, the company may well find that they have created a product that is not wanted or needed on a wide scale. When educational systems are judged by one set of standards or one performance indicator (such as a state standardized test), they become producers of Stepford children without the range of skills that the world may demand of them. The following excerpt from the Website <www.kidsource.com>[4] takes the concept of judging a school on the basis of its tests one step further. This Website, established for parents by parents, indicates that one of the primary publics associated with a school may not approve of the methodologies used to indicate success!

> Teachers feel compelled to spend considerable time preparing children to take the tests. In such cases, the tests become the school curriculum. Preparation usually begins many weeks before actual testing. During this period, two to three hours a day are often devoted to practicing tests and related exercises, all alien to the ongoing instruction and the usual student response patterns. Teachers readily

acknowledge that questions in the practice exercises, which are similar to those on the real test, are trivial. Moreover, the possible responses contain words that children likely have never seen and certainly don't use. By the time the three days of real testing are over, weeks, sometimes months, have passed. Time for real books has been sacrificed for time spent reading isolated paragraphs and answering multiple-choice questions. Time has been spent not on posing problems for which math might be used, and in the process coming to a natural understanding of math concepts, but on reviewing skills such as addition, subtraction, and division—all in isolation.

Teaching to the test is a whispered phrase in public school hallways. Heated discussions take place over selling our scholastic souls for a test score. And for what purposes? Overall, corporations are not indicating dissatisfaction with the skill levels of today's workers. They are not experiencing problems with the knowledge base of their employees. Primarily, they are requesting that schools do a more proficient job of creating a worker who can interact cooperatively with others and solve problems by using complex reasoning skills. Author Alfie Kohn speaks of two camps of education, "educating for profit" and "educating for democracy." He discusses the purposes of corporate concern for and involvement in public schools. He states, "On the one hand, there are humanistic goals: helping children become contented and fulfilled, helping them grow into adults with a deeper understanding of themselves and the world around them. On the other hand, there are more utilitarian goals, such as helping children grow into adults with lots of money."[5] As we step into the twenty-first century, we are going to find that both qualities must be present, but without the former, the latter will mean very little.

In a journal article, Wisconsin's former State Superintendent of Schools, John Benson, places the following characteristics on equal footing with state standards: *Promoting Core Values, Ensuring a Safe Environment, Involving Families and the Community, Developing Positive Relationships, Addressing Societal Issues, Engaging Students' Minds,* and *Having High Expectations.*[6] Benson indicates that these are "of equal importance" to the development of academic standards. Unfortunately, students did not find a place to show an accomplishment of these on their last standardized test.

Who is going to tell the village that raises the child all that the tests don't measure? Bill Ayers, an educator, summed it up well. He said, "Standardized tests can't measure initiative, creativity, imagination, conceptual thinking, curiousity, effort, irony, judgement, commitment, nuance, good will, ethical reflection, or a host of other valuable dispositions and attributes."[7]

A WALK THROUGH THE VILLAGE

The expectation that education can be standardized poses an ethical question that forces us to take a hard look at the village. Let's start with the fulfillment of basic needs—food and shelter. Approximately four million American children under age 12 go hungry and about 9.6 million more are at risk of hunger according to estimates based on the results of the most comprehensive study ever done on childhood hunger in the United States—the Community Childhood Hunger Identification Project (CCHIP). Based on the results of over 5,000 CCHIP surveys of families with incomes below 185 percent of poverty, applied to the best available national data, the Food Research and Action Center (FRAC) estimates that approximately 13.6 million children under age 12 in the United States— 29 percent—live in families who must cope with hunger or the risk of hunger during some part of one or more months of the previous year.[8] How many of that 29 percent are going to have the time and the energy to focus on the education of children?

Consider the following facts on homelessness as offered by the National Alliance to End Homelessness:

> 750,000 Americans are homeless on any given night. Over the course of a year, as many as 2 million people experience homelessness for some period of time.

The fastest growing group of homeless people consists of families with children. Today, families make up about 36% of the people who become homeless. The typical homeless family consists of a young unmarried mother with two or three small children. Many of these young mothers are fleeing domestic violence, and most lack the work skills, access to child care, or access to jobs necessary to support their families. (*A Status Report on Hunger and Homelessness in America's Cities: 1997*, U.S. Conference of Mayors, December 1997)[9]

Consider the overwhelming data on poverty and again ask the village to invest in its children. Ask them to make informed decisions about the curriculum. Ask them if the standards impact their lives. Which do you think will be more meaningful to them . . . food on the table, gas in the car, or the fact that Johnny isn't doing all thirty of his math problems every night? Beyond that, think of the children themselves and the priority of education in light of these statistics offered by the National Center for Children in Poverty.

America's children are more likely to live in poverty than Americans in any other age group. During the past two decades there has been a substantial increase in the number and percentage of poor children under age 18 in the United States.

- Over 11 million children live in poverty and *the number of children living in poverty has increased by 3 million since 1979*. The child poverty rate grew by 15 percent from 1979 to 1998.

- *16 percent of children live in poverty*, i.e., in families with incomes below the federal poverty line ($13,861 for a family of three in 1998).

- *The United States' child poverty rate is substantially higher*—often two-to-three times higher—than that of most other major Western industrialized nations.

- *While the child poverty rate is highest for African American* (30 percent) *and Latino* (28 percent) *children,* by international standards *it is also exceptionally high for white children* (9 percent).

• *6 percent of America's children live in extreme poverty,* in families with incomes below 50 percent of the poverty line. (In 1998, the extreme poverty line was $6,430 for a family of three.) Research indicates that extreme poverty during the first five years of life has especially deleterious effects on children's future life chances compared to less extreme poverty experienced later in childhood.

• Finally, *37 percent of American children live in or near poverty,* in families with incomes below 200 percent of the poverty line ($27,722 for a family of three). Many of the concerns of "near poor" families overlap with those of the poor, e.g., the need for well-paying jobs and access to affordable quality child care and health care.[10]

Public schools are also experiencing a rapidly emerging effect from the onslaught of divergent cultures resulting from trends in immigration to the United States. Immigrant groups are most highly affected by poverty, and school dropout rates are dramatically influenced by factors such as language acquisition for students and families, pre-existing cultural biases as to the importance of education, and a lack of funding and support for appropriate transitory English as a Second Language (ESL) programs in public schools across the United States. As a result, the ability of foreign-born children to first graduate and then participate in a competitive job market is severely skewed.

Admittedly, until it happened to me, I was quite sheltered on the issues associated with the language needs of children. I was working in a school that had little cultural diversity. Our foreign-born students generally had functional English skills before arriving at the middle school. Of course, there were the difficulties associated with any communications sent home but our teachers handled these individually with finesse. So, I was not really ready the day that Miguel and Monica stepped into my office with their father.

I had already met Mr. Garcia. He had come in and through a blend of his English and my hit-and-miss Spanish, we had already spent a few hours together filling out enrollment papers for his children. He told me that they spoke no English but I thought that he meant that they, like him, struggled with fluency. He meant that they spoke NO English.

I started out with "Hi" and a shy smile. They returned both. So far so good. I smiled harder and said, "You will like our school." They smiled harder, too, their eyes reflecting no understanding. "You will both be in seventh grade and have the same teacher." The smiles lessened and became strained. All of them. Their eyes continued to be mystified. "We will help you learn English." At the mention of the word *English* their eyes lit up and they nodded. I could feel my voice growing louder and my already basic speech more pronounced. I smiled at their eager hope and gave them the most quiet school tour that I have ever given. When they left, I put my head down on my desk and sighed. Two weeks until school would start. We had no English as a Second Language teacher and no resources to hire one. We had a K–12 specialist who worked half time to address the language needs of students. It wasn't enough. I went home and dug through my son's long-forgotten books and books on tape in storage and hoped that two weeks from Monday would not be the day that a group of well-intentioned policy makers and their media counterparts would swoop down upon my school and make measure of the standards.

The Census Bureau has reported that the country's Hispanic population increased by 58 percent from 1990 to 2000—making it the fastest growing minority group—and underscoring "the changing diversity of the United States."[11] Increased multiculturalism has definite effects on the American classroom. Increased diversity perpetuates the necessity of providing translators, bilingual teachers, modified curricula, and outreach efforts for Hispanic parents. All over America, dedicated teachers are doing whatever it takes to make certain that all students in their classrooms receive a free public education. They are doing it without increased time and often without increased resources. I personally know a seventh-grade teacher who spends many of her evening hours typing her lessons for the next day into a free translator program that is available on the Internet so that her newest Hispanic student can follow along. Luckily, her student is literate in his own language and can grasp the basics due to her extra efforts. But instead of lauding the efforts of this dedicated woman, the newspapers will seize the scores from the standardized test that she cannot rewrite.

Poverty, hunger, homelessness, and ethnicity are common elements of all cities in the United States. Yet policy makers and community leaders continue to judge the community and to make decisions based on their personal worldviews. It is surprising to know that when one looks at the world as a whole, 50 percent of people have never made or received a phone call. In the United States, 8 percent of children live in a house without a phone, 49 percent live in a house without a computer, and 73 percent live in a house without access to the Internet.[12]

I have a fantasy. I dream of the day that our president stands before the American people with his notes for his address in his hand. It is my vision that those notes would be in a language that our president does not speak nor read. There would be a test at the end for all of the policy makers in the audience. Any educational policy maker not passing would have his or her salary reduced with the new available monies going to better servicing the language needs of the minority children in our schools. I know that it probably won't come to fruition, but even an overworked teacher can dream.

A CALL TO ACTION

Education reform efforts that are not reflective of all the factors impacting a school cannot be successful and ultimately will serve only to weaken the system as a whole. No one would expect a business to create a quality product using only one set of controls. The perfect pizza cannot be manufactured accurately on faulty machinery. It cannot be packaged correctly without ergonomic design. It cannot be transported appropriately without temperature controls. When experts fail to consider all aspects of production when likening schools to businesses, they wreak havoc on the system.

Rudyard Kipling is famous for his expression of each person's inter-reliance on others. He says, "The strength of the wolf is the pack . . . and the strength of the pack is the wolf."[13] Indeed, the same can be said for the village. The individuals within the village can positively contribute to school reform. The community as a whole can reflect a commitment to the success of its schools. But this can only happen when the schools and the children are viewed for the unique entity that they are; a corporation is a cold and imposing structure—a school is an extended family.

CHAPTER TWO

TO MARKET, TO MARKET

Good marketing is essential to the corporate world. It is also increasingly essential to public schools. This chapter examines the underpinnings of this trend, as well as the unique challenges faced by public schools as they attempt to become more savvy "retailers" of their educational products.

AND THE WINNER IS...

Any good marketing program protocol has, as a basic tenet, a dictum that marketing strategies align with consumer needs. This leads us to ask a pivotal question for public schools...just who is our consumer?

Purists argue that the child is the ultimate consumer. Thus, the single-minded creation of child-centered learning environments ought to satisfy consumer demand. However, real-world application disproves this theory. As with real-world marketing, the child has only certain powers as a viable consumer. He is not a wage earner, nor is he considered the best source of guidance for the programs at his disposal. Indeed, if children were left to govern themselves, schools may well be filled with video games and soda machines, right? Or perhaps music, discovery, laughter, and technology. Hmmm... perhaps providing students with a sense of their own consumerism is not so ludicrous as it, at first, seems. The ultimate goal of the new paradigm of education is that of students as their own products, continuously improving, getting better and better and helping others do the same.[1]

Then again, the school is in *loco parentis*, or, to put it simply, is there to serve in the role of the child's parent during the hours of school operation. Should not an agency that speaks for the parent be in the employ of the parent? Abraham Lincoln may have written his own speeches, but today's political figures hire those who can express most articulately their particular philosophies. In this same light, don't parents engage educational professionals to enact a curriculum that most suitably meets their child's needs? In this case, then, the parent becomes the primary consumer of the school. Each character in the school scene is responding to a different set of cues even as they act on the same stage. The wise school strives to find a balance between the two.

Schools are supported by tax dollars. Only 36 percent of households have children under the age of 18 living in them and that includes families who pay rent rather than property taxes.[2] Predictably, then, the remaining school funding comes largely from other taxpayers within the community. This vast population of the consumers associated with a school may well be the most difficult to satisfy and because of their size, they may be the most influential group as well.

ONE FOR YOU..., TWO FOR ME

Where then are the limited marketing dollars available in our schools to go? Those living on the fringe of meaningful educational engagement care more for results than process, while the consumers "in the trenches" care more about the day-to-day interactions that affect their lives with immediacy. This is most obvious in the corollary of quality improvement that states that activities within an organization must be planned, implemented, and evaluated. Never can the door of the process close so that the procedures can be evaluated. We cannot stop the process of educating children to determine if that education is being effective. We can't shut down the machines of production without having new machines ready to replace them. In short, it is difficult to assess and to satisfy the requirements of the results-oriented community while in the process of procuring those results. Remember that childhood experience of trying to jump onto the merry-go-round while it was in motion? Reaping and articulating the results that demonstrate quality is much like that process.

EIGHTY PERCENT OF TIME FOR TWENTY PERCENT OF PEOPLE

Be advised that this does not mean that quality results are not present. The ineffective handling of marketing by schools is a multiheaded monster. But the immediate faces of danger are both money and time.

Consider Microsoft. As with the constancy of the world of education, technology operates under Moire's law that stipulates that "technology doubles itself every six months." Anyone who has purchased a home computer has felt the hand of the grim reaper on his shoulder, knowing that they are buying a product whose time has already come. Yet one does not see long lines of complainants trailing to the streets surrounding the computer production factories or even read much press associated with the trend. Instead, we seem to have a passé acceptance of *caveat emptor* and to take the principles of technology in our stride. Money and time. How much of both do you think Microsoft spends on its own marketing?

As educators, we spend too much time, energy, and money trying to reach people who are unlikely to change their opinions about public education. Consider this. A third of a school's consumers are consistent supporters, a third are on the fence, and a third hold largely unchangeable views regarding public education. Yet we continue to aim our best marketing ploys at those in the negative third. The positive and the negative thirds will often seek out school personnel for two-way communication. The middle third tends to be more passive observers. Schools should narrow their marketing focuses and concentrate on drawing in the middle third of the people.[3] Hillshire probably doesn't advertise in *Vegetarian* magazine. Think about it.

IT'S A SMALL WORLD, AFTER ALL

So far, we've discussed three main consumers that a singular school may have. But what about the concept of developing "World Citizens"? The information superhighway allows for fast travel around the world. This means that our students must no longer be prepared to grow up and live only in Mayberry, but in Tokyo, Prague, Paris, and Versailles. While it seems a stretch at an immediate level, the consumer of any education is inevitably the world that receives the outcome of that education.

We've discussed the quandary of defining a singular consumer of an education. In recent years, business marketers have attempted to provide clarity by defining their own consumers within the educational realm.

Our school has Channel One, the marketing brainstorm that hit schools in 1989. Channel One Communications (then Whittle Communications) offered to provide school districts with up to $50,000 in "free" electronic equipment including televisions, VCRs, and satellite dishes on the condition that 90 percent of the students watch the ten-minute news broadcast each day that school is in session. Sounds like a pretty good deal, right? The news is well done and kid-friendly. Who couldn't use a better handle on current events? But the program each day is twelve minutes long. That's two minutes of commercials designed for a captive student audience.

My school has Channel One. One day during the second week of school, Channel One didn't tape properly. A student in fifth-hour science captured the miracle of advertising best when he quipped, "That's OK. I can do the Gatorade ad for all

17

of us." He stood up at his seat and mimed a sweaty athlete taking a soothing drink. I guess it's true that the students are always learning. Sometimes, though, I wonder what we're teaching them.[4,5]

Consider the cover story in *Business Week* that reported on the adoption of a McDonald's-sponsored curriculum package. Commenting on what one ten-year-old student learned from the curriculum, *Business Week* claimed that

> Travis Licata recently learned how to design a McDonald's restaurant, how a McDonald's works, and how to apply and interview for a job at McDonald's thanks to [the] seven week company sponsored class intended to teach kids about the work world. When Travis was asked if the curriculum was worthwhile, he responded, "If you want to work in a McDonald's when you grow up, you already know what to do . . . Also, McDonald's is better than Burger King."[6]

Students who look at book covers with company logos, scoreboards that promote soft drinks, and marketing banners on the outsides and insides of school buses are being sent the message that everything has a price. The ads don't show the third-world workers who struggle without labor laws to create the product. They don't explain about capitalism and hidden agendas. Is it altruism that drives corporations to make "free" donations to schools in the name of curriculum? The catastrophe of the *Exxon Valdez* oil spill is muted by Exxon's video on the issue of environmental protection. The history of the potato chip is made relevant by curricular contributions from the Potato Board and Snack Food Association. Geothermal eruptions occur as students pop "Gushers" fruit snacks in their mouths courtesy of General Mills.[7] Grandma always said there was no such thing as a free lunch, but maybe if schools start to parcel their allegedly free contributions into food groups, there could be.

We of logical mind shake our fists at the corporate manipulation of children. Little do we realize that we, too, are targets of the marketers' middle fingers. My son came home from his first day of fifth grade lugging with him the usual myriad of forms and information. Interestingly, there was also a flyer from Express gas stations. It seems that for every eight gallons of gas

purchased at an Express convenience center, the school receives
$1.60. Of course, it means getting stamps and keeping receipts
and hoping that they don't somehow wind up in the laundry
before making their way to the mailbox. It also means buying
fuel at Express. Just who is being benevolent to whom?

The local grocery store chains want a piece of the action, too.
And the soup people. And the box top brigade. And the local
mall. The school district Web page leads me to three online sites
that offer a great many stores and catalogs. If I make a purchase
from any of these places, my child's school gets a kickback. And
what does the kindly corporation receive? Profits and tax write-
offs and the warm glow of aiding education. And profits and
tax write-offs. But we shop at the stores and buy our gas where
we are "supposed" to. We even implore grandma and grandpa
and hordes of relatives to do the same. We do it for the sake
of the children. From our pocketbooks to the corporate table.
And the scraps fall to the children. Alex Molnar says it best, "If
the current trend continues, the link between the provision of
public education and the ability of schools to deliver corporate
profits could be irrevocable by the end of the century."[8] It is
already the new millenium. Let's hope we are not too late.

A PIGGY BANK OF TIME

Another basic tenet of marketing states that once a consumer
field is identified, it is up to the agency to find a balance between marketing strategies. We have already touched on the
dynamics that impact this, namely, diversity, money, and time.
Education has become creative over the years, employing programs that strive not only to serve an increasingly diverse
student population, but to effectively merge all consumers integral to education with that service. From this effort, service
learning, child mentoring, school-to-work partnerships, and efforts such as those put out by Junior Achievement were born. All
of these efforts sport the basic belief in the value of education,
all have noble aspirations for the betterment of youth, and all

are as tenuous as the grants or the "people power" that supports them.

So why do we allow such slip-shod enactment of even our best educational tools? We return again to time and money. Mentoring a child, for example, takes time. I helped to establish and administer a mentoring program for a school district for over three years. It meant an added investment of at least five hours of time each week. In the first year of the program, we had students requesting mentors simply because they saw the relationships that their peers were developing. In the second year, I had a student previously written off as at-risk of not graduating from high school express a very real desire and commitment to go to college. By the end of the third year, the program espoused measurable results: having an adult mentor from the community increased attendance, decreased office referrals, and raised grades. No one from the business community wore their corporate logos. No one asked to be part of a publicity shot. In fact, anonymous donations to the school and to individual families in need increased instead. The business community saw the need for time and gave it. In the third year, they even established after-school study help for students at the elementary and middle schools. Was it worth my time? Undoubtedly. But sadly, all it would take for such a program to crumble is the absence of somebody's time.

Let's not forget about money. Many of our best programs in the public schools are supported by whimsical grant dollars. There are grants dedicated to making schools drug free. In some schools, monies targeted for this purpose go towards providing each student with an agenda for homework organization and home communication. The agenda is a pricey necessity and many families would not be able to afford to provide one for their children. So the grant writers got creative (a prerequisite for grant writers everywhere) and they noted that the nice folks at the agenda company were willing to put a page in the agenda promoting healthy lifestyles. *Voilà!* What a sad commentary that schools are forced to choose which best practice to use this year. Drug-free curricula or home communication tools? The idea is akin to being forced to eat from just one food group. And this time the scraps are falling from the Federal table.

ON YOUR MARK, GET SET, GOAL!

Think back to the tour of the pizza plant mentioned in the introductory pages of this book. The output of 7000 pizzas per hour was an achievable and measurable goal. Having accomplished it, shift workers could feel good not only about their own performance, but that of their entire working team. In short, business often has short-term, readily quantifiable goals that indicate its success.

What are the short-term goals of the public school? That Jimmy learn to read? That Julie not get pregnant? That Willie get a winter coat and a morning meal? That Javier learn to communicate? That all teachers of mathematics are on page 73 of the textbook on the very same day?

Ask any good teacher about goals and you will hear things related to learning, classroom climate, and meeting the just-in-time (JIT) needs of students. In a concentrated effort by politicians masked as marketers, teachers have been asked to esteem more than this. It is not enough to have students learning, we are told. But they must learn "measurable content standards." Discussions about the creation of a positive classroom climate are dismissed. It is simply expected that the magic of entering a classroom door will allow students of a pluralistic society that cannot get along with one another to be comfortable and cooperative with one another. I would like to invite all politicians and CEOs to an elementary cafeteria at lunch time. After watching the students mash bananas into their fists, miss their mouths with spaghetti, and laugh uproariously over bodily functions, perhaps those who dismiss the creation of climate and the teaching of the social skills necessary to establishing that climate might have a different perspective.

While few outside the realm of public education want to hear about the "soft skills" that comprise a good deal of the informal curricula, even fewer want to comprehend the educational significance of the just-in-time meeting of student needs. A teacher is responsible not only to the academic curriculum but also to the micromanagement of a plethora of loosely related tasks. They provide Band-Aids to boo-boos, advice to the lovelorn, message services to students about pickups and dropoffs and dentist appointments. They send students out for special services, receive them in for mainstreamed instruction, and send them out again for band, remedial reading, English as a Second Language services, guidance counselor appointments, and speech therapy. And with the countenance of a harried Yellow Cab dispatcher, they forge ahead with decimals and the basics of the nebular theory.

The just-in-time meeting of student needs does not end at the close of the work day. Those who envy the schedule of a teacher have obviously not lived it. The JIT needs extend far beyond the academic to the practical. Teachers carry huge stacks of work home each night, so that correcting in class does not take the place of curriculum. Teachers go to Goodwill and hunt for a sweatshirt for Paul, a warm jacket for Jan, and mittens for Sarah. Teachers telephone the parents of their students, often after both parties have tucked small children into bed for the night. In the mornings, they are roused by insistent alarms just in time to do it all again.

MARKET: COUNTERMARKET

Somewhere near the time that *A Nation at Risk*[9] was published, public school officials realized the importance of bringing the many positive happenings within the walls of their schools to the public eye. Since that time, schools have been poised to "countermarket" the negative publicity that seems to follow the United States educational system like a shadow of doom.

Consider the effect of these potent words from *The New York Times,* which quizzed students on key facts about their country. "A large majority of students showed that they had virtually no knowledge of elementary aspects of American history. They could not identify such names as Abraham Lincoln, Thomas Jefferson, Andrew Jackson, or Theodore Roosevelt. Most of our students do not have the faintest idea what this country looks like."

It is exactly rhetoric like this that President Bush has in mind when he talks about our current "education recession." There is only one caveat yet to add . . . these words appeared in the April 4, 1943, edition of the *Times*.[10] Clearly, the idea that bad news sells faster than good news is not a new one.

Armed with the knowledge that good things were happening each day in our nation's schools, educators began to invest their already precious commodities of time and money into the promotion of positive school practices. When I became a middle school principal, it was important to me to generate positive publicity for our school. I developed a press release policy and I cultivated relationships with local media agencies. In a concentrated effort, our middle school received some positive press. Only once in my six-year experience did I have anyone outside of the educational realm be impressed with this. It seems all the "feel good" marketing in the world ultimately will make only the marketer and the direct participants truly feel good.

School–media relations have become a proverbial "dog and pony show." Educators seek to highlight the best and the brightest students, the boldest new innovations, or those educational programs that demonstrate an emotional investment in less fortunate youth. We want to showcase the vast uses of technologies in our schools, detail the strengths of our newest curricular bandwagons, and impress our publics with our displays of tolerance, service, and civic responsibility. We are a bit like the smallest puppy at the pound, wanting to prove our worthiness and be adopted by public approval.

I certainly never called the local newspaper and told them about all the JIT meeting of needs that was going on at our school. I never called to report how many students had field trips funded from the pockets of caring teachers. I didn't fax the story the day that I taught a sixth-grade girl how to wash her hair and cleanse her body . . . not even after the joy of seeing her marvel at her "new" reflection in the mirror. Not even when she came back into the office to ask if she could look at herself again. I didn't dash off a press release on the morning when Arturo finally smiled and said "good morning" to me in broken English. It was his first successful phrase. And his first real smile.

Having the story wedged on page 17 of the local paper on a slow news day would have altered the celebration of the moment. But that is not why I didn't call.

Schools rarely report their realities and the school–business model is largely to blame. We don't tell the good we do for the needy in our charge because the very presence of those children detracts from the marketable image of a school. Years of corporate advertising has taught consumers to focus only on the major message of any given ad strategy. It would be economic suicide for a food producing company to advertise that they had successfully eradicated their problem with rodents. The public trust is most comfortable when it can have both blinders and expectations. That is, the public does not wish to be disheartened with the threats to the security of the enterprises they support and they wish to keep their expectations visible at all times through rose-colored glasses. Media revels in the business of removing blinders and in the shock-value of dashing expectations. Schools that are too honest about the harsh realities facing the students in their classrooms walk a precariously fine line between being viewed as saviors or institutions in need of salvation. It is not a risk most schools choose to take.

WOULDN'T YOU LIKE TO BE A PEPPER, TOO?

A link to the business model and risk are not the only factors that preclude public schools from effectively informing and marketing to their publics. The variance of those publics and the effects of a constantly changing culture are among other crucial factors that make appropriate school marketing both difficult and incomparable to corporate marketing.

I reached for a can of Coca-Cola the other day. I like Coke. I've liked it since I was about six years old. It hasn't changed much. Same red can. Same fizz. Same taste. Other than that little indiscretion of trying to make a new cola out of a namesake, the basic product that accompanies my lunch has not changed much over the last thirty years. The basic product and its quantifiable expectation of performance have not been altered by a changing society. Poverty, homelessness, cultural difficulties, violence, discrimination, and educational standards do little to affect the taste of my Coke. The same cannot be said for the "product" of American schools . . . its children.

Schools cannot create a product that will sell itself in the same manner from year to year. To think of doing so decade to decade is ludicrous. Corporations continually express the desire to hire technologically adept personnel who possess higher-level thinking skills and cooperative leadership abilities. Education faces the awesome task of creating the workers of tomorrow. To look at human beings as a product that can be standardized and marketed is to make them a commodity and not a community.

Corporate marketing always relies on four tenets: product, promotion, place, and price. As discussed, schools have little control over the raw materials or over many of the environmental ingredients that will affect the finished product. Promotion has taken on a feel-good quality that has a positive impact only on those who already support public school programs. In fact, too much positive promotion can actually inhibit the development of programs that work for students. Schools that are on the cutting edge of technology may be perceived as having "arrived" and thus be viewed as less in need of continued financial support. Schools that publicize their thriving mentoring programs may be taxed with increasingly long waiting lists of needy students (because the public perception will be that the need for mentors has been filled). Schools that extol the virtues of cooperative learning within their walls may soon find themselves at the mercy of a group of parents who oppose such educational strategies.

This morning, I heard on the radio that the American Civil Liberties Union (ACLU) is requesting that an elementary school in California remove its patriotic "God Bless America" sign from the lawn of its school, placed there in a postterrorism display of citizenship. The cry of "separation of church and state" could be heard before the paint on the sign could dry. Schools today cannot be too political, too patriotic, too conservative, too liberal, or too tolerant. And apparently they also cannot be too careful.

PLEASE, SIR, I WANT SOME MORE

In the jargon of corporate marketing, the word *place* describes a method of product distribution. Loosely aligned to education, the perceived counterpart of place would be the means of curriculum distribution. White boards have replaced chalkboards, keyboards have retired typewriters, and the Internet has triumphed over the Dewey Decimal System. In most states, Big Brother has drawn his penknife and whittled the curriculum down to standardized components that can fit into cozy cubbyholes. But the students who stand at the boards, run their fingers over the keyboards, and surf the Net cannot be standardized quite so neatly.

Imagine if the ingredients back at the pizza factory had to be placed on a pizza before its time. Haphazard lumps of sausage atop cheeseless and sauceless crust would hardly be a saleable product. Instead, the production is carefully supervised and the pizzas that come off the line are able to be distributed without fear to waiting markets.

There are waiting markets for students, too, and they are as diverse as the learners themselves. An Ivy League college, a blue-collar industry, a cutting-edge technological firm, a branch of the U.S. military, or a technical school will all have different expectations of the candidates seeking affiliation with them. How far is it appropriate to stretch school dollars to educate every individual for the aspect of the adult world they will enter? How feasible is it to imagine that all students graduating high school will even have a clear picture of their ultimate career goals?

The answer, of course, is to shoot for the middle and hope to hit enough basic academic and affective skills to satisfy a broad range of markets. This cannot be done in the corporate world. Competition creates a consistent pattern of "one-upmanship" and more refined products. Consumers want the very best item to meet their needs and not a reasonably good item that may leave some gaps in their expectation. Gaps in expectation will always lead to some level of dissatisfaction. When business and political moguls consider America's children an ultimate product of the public educational system, there will always be a criticism waiting in the wings. Perhaps it is time to simply stop inviting it on stage.

It is time for those in charge of educational marketing to realize that they are not selling something. Curriculum is not a commodity. Learning is not a repossessible possession. Endeavoring to create world citizens with qualities of character is not done for a camera or a newspaper or for applause. Teachers are public servants dedicated to the public good. They do not teach skills that will be a luxury to have in the future. They teach what is necessary to ensure that there is a future.

CHAPTER THREE

A ROSE BY ANY OTHER NAME

Educational standards are often imposed by incidental players on the field of public education. Yet, they hold incredible power. This chapter examines the impact of the standards movement on students, teachers, and subsequently on the publics that schools serve.

WHERE IS THE LORAX NOW?

We need someone to speak for the trees! Tongue in cheek? Only partly.

I was at a team meeting the other day where the topic of discussion was an administrative dictum that the curricular standards employed each week in the classroom be documented. I use the term *discussion* loosely because people were angry. Not only had the standards been dissected and documented only recently at a staff development day but they had been matched to year-long curriculum in both of the previous school years, too. It wasn't long before the inevitable question arose, "And when do they want me to teach?"

I've been on both sides of the table. I've been a "they." And I was a "they" who wanted our school's teachers to spend time instructing students instead of scribbling curriculum coordinates on an unending plethora of maps and grids and charts. But the powers that hold the purse strings are imposing, too. In a time of blame and litigation it seems there can never be quite enough protection or accountability. So we weave blankets of curriculum jargon with just enough verbiage to cover our seats and we let our hearts grow cold.

Accountability is not a bad word. Unfortunately, it has become a buzzword. Its significance and that of educational standards are undermined by the paranoia inherent in the expectation that a public school must create an assembly line product. Public schools are and must continue to be responsible in instructing students. A quality curriculum reflects not only the academic basics that are necessary for living fulfilled adult lives but also instills character, competence in technology, and the metacognitive strategies necessary to solve complex problems. Author Alvin Toffler has said, "The illiterate of the year 2000 will not be the individual who cannot read and write, but the one who cannot learn, unlearn, and relearn." Schools must have an explicit agenda if they are to accomplish the awesome task facing them and it is important to be able to share with all publics affected by school performance precisely what the planned outcomes are for students.

Dr. W. Edward Deming, who is best known for his efforts on behalf of the Total Quality Management (TQM) model, is quoted as saying "You do not have to do this . . . survival is not compulsory." In the worst case scenario of the corporate world, this is true. The Swiss watchmakers who denounced the digital watch as a passing fad prove the veracity of Dr. Deming's statement. However, it is not true of public schools. Survival has been and always will be compulsory. Schools are literally dealing with the lifeblood of the future. There have always been standards present that keep the ever-growing body of knowledge available in our world vital and attainable.

So, what has changed? Why have politicians and corporate philosophers rolled up their shirtsleeves to stand poised with a proverbial pitchfork, ready to dig into the curriculum of America's schools? Perhaps the easiest answer is that *American Gothic* is a classic and by posturing to help the underdog of education, alleged benefactors present a portrait suitable for framing.

HE STARTED IT!

An administrator friend of mine often used the phrase "Deny! Deny! Deny!" The passing of the buck was somewhat of an expected tradition within the walls of our school. We jokingly referred to it as "The Shuffle." It would begin with that deer-in-the-headlights look and summate with a referral or a passing of the blame.

In the late 1980s, faced with a struggling economy and a series of financial snapshots each progressively more bleak than the last, the toes of corporate America started tapping. It was the beginning of a dance not unlike that of The Shuffle, but unlike the small scale blame-shifting that occurs within an agency, corporate powers allied themselves with political activists to shift America's focus to the deteriorating state of its public schools. In 1983, *A Nation at Risk* was born and, as with any birth, the brainchild of the National Commission of Excellence in Education became the focal point for both the appreciative and critical eye of the public. Capitalists everywhere rested easier in their four-poster beds! It was not myopic financial mismanagement that had caused the dire straits of the economy . . . it was the lack of appropriate education in America's schools! Fix the schools and fix the problem. Voilà!

In the practical sense, very few politicians or policy makers launched direct attacks on public schools. Instead, there was an avuncular, almost condescending, concern expressed in a series of "if onlys."

> If only schools could provide graduates who had the academic and social skills to be employed successfully in a competitive market.
>
> If only American schools could model themselves after the seemingly more evolved educational models of other countries.
>
> If only there were greater accountability and more concrete standards of performance.
>
> If only communities had more involvement in their schools.
>
> If only parents could make informed choices about the schools that their children would attend.

If only those choices could be funded by the involved community.

If only teachers would start doing more for less.

If only schools would employ solid management strategies with an eye on the bottom line.

If only schools were run more like businesses.

With a paternalistic air, policy makers assured schools that assistance was on the way. The public was assured that the curricular crises in schools would be solved. So effective was onslaught of deceptive research and misplaced forgiveness that even schools themselves began to see the world through the blurry lenses of the underdog. Public schools almost overnight became the needy instead of the needed. The carrot-and-stick approach is especially evident in the way that school programs are funded. Grant dollars? Government dollars? Corporate donations and gifts? All are sustainable by good behavior.

> Bully your partner from the side,
> pass the buck and shift the blame,
> Do–si–do and all join hands,
> Step in time and do it again.

WHOSE LINE IS IT ANYWAY?

Maggie was supposed to be learning the parts of speech and how to use context clues to improve her reading comprehension. She needed to know the elements of the short story. The standards were clear: rising action must be followed by a conflict before it could fall and conclude. Instead, she spent the first part of her reading class each day in my office.

I've seen the standards for Language Arts and Reading more times than I care to even ponder, and I know with full confidence that there is nothing about hygiene in them. There is nothing that told Maggie's classmates or her teacher how to cope with her unwashed hair, unbathed body, dirty clothes, and unbrushed teeth. There is nothing in the standards about students who smell like urine and animal waste, grease, and cigarette smoke. The standards don't address how to meet the needs of families so poor that the basics of human living become a daily struggle.

Maggie's family wanted better for her and for themselves. They had a questionable standard of cleanliness and couldn't often find the quarters that would precipitate loading their laundry into large bags and walking or biking it to the laundromat that was about two miles away. They assumed that their daughter's standards of health were acceptable because they aligned with their own. They figured that getting near the shower on a sporadic basis was all that was necessary for appropriate self-care. They ate the greased and starched diet of the poor, kept mangy pets that they could ill afford, and failed to ever oversee the using of a toothbrush within the household.

But they had a special shelf in the living room. Maggie told me about it. It was hers, all hers, in a house that fought itself for space to breathe. And they displayed Maggie's things there. Awards that her caring teachers had bestowed. Papers and projects she was proud of. School pictures, when they could afford them. With that shelf, they provided a foundation of caring that was Maggie's hope for attaining a better life.

But first, Maggie would have to be able to sit in class and not attract the negative attention of her peers. First, Maggie would have to learn to wash and dress and brush her teeth. Very literally, at twelve years of age, Maggie needed to learn all of these things. That's how Maggie ended up in my office.

One day, I just couldn't take it anymore. I didn't think about the standards as I drove home to get shampoo, soap, a blow dryer, a new toothbrush, and a change of clothing from the "used to fit me" section of my closet.

I knew that teaching Maggie to wash her hair and clean her body and brush her teeth wasn't going to satisfy the curriculum director's mandates. I knew that the basic life skills that Maggie was learning were not going to be measured on the state tests. And I knew that all those things she was supposed to be learning in reading class would.

But it was worth it. Maggie looked into the mirror and marveled at her clean hair. Her voice was at first soft, and then slightly concerned. "It's springy," she said, running her fingers through the brown layers. I reassured her that it was supposed to be and let her touch my hair as a model. She relaxed and continued to stare at her reflection. "I never knew my hair was brown," she said, because she was much more accustomed to the greasy black color that it often appeared. She smiled and thanked me and I invited her back each morning.

As Maggie was leaving the office, ready to return to reading to capture whatever fragments of the standards remained for that morning, she paused. She turned to look at me. And she asked the question that to this day mists my eyes with the tears of some people's lives. Her smile was shy and her voice was barely a whisper. "Could I go and look at my hair . . . just one more time?"

There are, literally, thousands of Maggies held within the collective arms of American public schools. There are subtle differences in the snapshots of their lives but the fact remains that the academic standards meant to equalize their education were not really written for them. They were not written for fourth-grader Joey who got the stomach flu at school and knew, by heart, the number of the bar where his mother could be reached at 10 A.M. She refused to pick him up from school.

The standards were not written for Jimmy, who, at age twelve, was the oldest in his family. Jimmy left school promptly each day so that he could go home and prepare dinner for his family while his mother worked two jobs. Jimmy worried more about laundry, homework, and making something besides cold cereal and macaroni and cheese for supper than he did about standards.

The standards were not written for Kim. In eighth grade, Kim confided to her guidance counselor that she was afraid to go home each day. Kim had the very realistic fear that she would soon find her uncontrolled, alcoholic mother dead on the kitchen floor as a result of alcohol poisoning. No one told Kim that failing to learn the geography of Brazil, the elements of the periodic table, and how to balance multistep equations might retain her indefinitely in eighth grade.

Standards are not the enemy, but inequitable conditions for learning are. Standards become the enemy when schools are given mandates without money, fear without focus, and expectation without anything extra. Jim Beane, a professor at National University and a well-known academic on the subject of middle-level education, spoke eloquently about standards as the enemy when he said, "Standards are not about democracy, but about Social Darwinism. They are about those with the most cultural capital doing the best on the tests."[1]

> Our schools have been consumed by a cult of measurement, which has blinded Americans to real damage. And it has blinded us to a sense of our own history: We keep repeating the same mistakes. At the Education Writers Association annual conference in Atlanta earlier this year, panelists (I was one of them) were asked whether the new breed of high-stakes testing "will doom minority children to sanctions." Given the ignominious history of mental testing in the United States, it's amazing that journalists can still ask such a question with a straight face. The answer is abundantly clear and has been so for a very long time.
>   The losers in high-stakes testing schemes always have been children of the poor, the working class and undereducated. And the winners always have been children of the privileged, well educated and the affluent.
>   From the U.S. Army's use of IQ tests at the turn of the century to categorize some recent immigrants as "feeble minded," to the high school graduation tests and district retention schemes we see from Chicago to North Carolina, government-mandated use of mental tests has always served to further stratify the nation along race, ethnic and class lines.[2]

A recent National Study of middle school principals' responses to the impact of standards within their educational environments, may, at first, make it seem as though the standards are indeed the panacea that public schools have needed. However, there are some critical reflections that data alone cannot deliver. First, the fact that this is an administrative rather than a teaching response is crucial. I have been an administrator. A large part of my job was marketing and politicking. It is always easier to market and speak to a singular product. Standards provide a tidy product. At last, the focus of the public eye can be shifted from the divergence found between classrooms. At last, schools can offer packaged proof that their students are being offered a curriculum that will match the tests that they will someday be required to take. At last, the "feel good" curriculum is being replaced by rigor and responsibility. Or is it?

THE UNDERCOVER CURRICULUM

The real curriculum is what occurs within the four walls of a classroom. All of the standards in the world, no matter how fashionably they are dressed, will not get through a door if that teacher does not invite them in. No one goes into the field of education to "do it someone else's way." Teachers are thinking professionals who will not abide mandates that don't suit their goals. They will jump through hoops. They will write the reams of flow charts and outcomes that their district administrators require. And they will return to their classrooms, shut their doors, and do what works most effectively for kids. And some, unfortunately, will do what works most effectively for themselves. But in either scenario, the standards will have been replaced by the substance of education . . . the heart and mind of the classroom teacher.

When I was a new teacher, I had the opportunity to receive part of my teaching certification "on the job." My university professor was an extreme advocate of the direct instruction method of teaching learning disabled students. I was not. He expressed his dismay after his first visit to my classroom and gave me the directive of change. And I did change. When he next visited me, my students could read from the board as I tapped on vocabulary words in beautiful harmony. What he did not see were the candy bar payoffs that I gave them when he left. Curriculum is always what occurs within the four walls of a classroom.

Another critical reflection of the national study of the standards is the knowledge that educators are just at the onset of taming the standards. New programs require directed energies and scores of time. The amount of focus necessary to put all

35

of the standards through all of the governmental paces will be unsustainable. The fact that 41 percent of school administrators feel that the standards are producing a negative effect on school climate cannot be ignored. In fact, it may well be the most alarming statistic revealed by the study.[3] Parker Palmer, author of *The Courage to Teach* [4], states that "we teach who we are." In stressful times of paperwork accountability and a "stay within the lines" approach to curriculum, "who we are" loses not only professionalism, but also creativity, energy, and quality. Beyond that, the education profession loses people. A university instructor was lamenting this sad fact at a recent conference. "I used to have people call to ask advice on how to become a better teacher," he said, "now I have them calling to ask what other professions they could transition into."

THE TOM SAWYER APPROACH

There will, of course, always be teachers. But will there be enough? The Council of Great City Schools is comprised of 57 large city school districts. Its mission is to promote the cause of urban schools and to advocate for the needs of inner-city youth. In a report released in January of 2000, the Recruiting New Teachers, Inc. (RNTI) agency conveyed that the Great City Schools serve 6.5 million students of whom 40 percent are African American, 30 percent are Hispanic, 21 percent are white, 6.4 percent are Asian/Pacific Islander, and 0.6 percent are Alaskan/Native American. Just over 60 percent of students are eligible for free/reduced lunch, 21 percent are English language learners, and 11.4 percent are students with individual education programs.[5]

The efforts of the RNTI indicate that there is an immediate and ongoing demand for teachers, especially teachers of color, male teachers, and bilingual teachers. In addition, special needs, science, and math continue to be areas in need of qualified educators.

The standards movement assures that demand will always outpace need. Attracting teachers to needy urban areas has always been a struggle. And now, in addition to the stresses already present in delivering a quality curriculum to a group of students with diverse and immediate nonacademic needs, teachers face fear, uncertainty, and shame.

In a workshop that I was conducting on character education, I had teachers attending from across the United States. One bright, animated woman began to tell the group about her school. She lowered her eyes. Her voice got softer and a blush reached her cheek. She was barely audible when she reported that hers was a school in the second year of a remediation program because of the poor performance of students on standardized tests. My heart went out to her. Her caring and her professionalism were expressed in shame and dismay. She felt powerless. And why shouldn't she? Each day she did her professional best within a situation that she did not create and she was still told that her efforts, and those of her colleagues, were not good enough. She worked every day with the fear that if the students couldn't learn more, faster, and retain it until the time of the testing, that she would lose her job. She wondered where there was time to teach respect and fairness and responsibility within the growing body of academic expectations. I posed the question to the group: "And what is the worst possible outcome of teaching character first?" The answer was a sad statement on behalf of education: "We'll lose our jobs."

Professions that involve high amounts of fear, shame, or uncertainty are generally not attractive. At the very least, professions that involve high amounts of stress are generally well respected and well compensated. Teaching is neither of these. Urban districts spend valuable district dollars on recruiting good teachers. They recruit at historically Black and Hispanic colleges, offer on-the-spot contracts, monetary bonuses, loan forgiveness programs, financial assistance for graduate schooling, and alternative certification routes. But whitewashing fences is hard work. Eventually, even the bait is not worth the bite. Standards that stymie creativity, encourage rigidity, and replace high expectations with fear shortchange public schools by denying them continued access to quality teaching professionals. Without an outpouring of empathy, support, and respect, an already narrow pool of candidates will dry completely.

EFFICIENT INEFFICIENCIES

Madeline Hunter and Bloom's Taxonomy. Say these two phrases in any room full of educators and immediately there will be a straightening of spines and the glazed-over look of remembering lesson plans created with more regimen than boot camp troops on graduation day. Standards, in their purest form, have been used by educators for years. Innocent standards, the ones not imposed by a Big Brother mentality, have always served to bind objectives together and make outcomes happen.

Educators have always had the tools of vision, organization, rigor, and high expectation and they have used these tools to transition students most appropriately into the decades they would inherit as adults. The more subtle standards focused on the growing of people instead of the simple raising of a body of knowledge. In *Education Week,* Robert Reich had this to say about today's new standards: "Paradoxically, we're embracing standardized tests when the new economy is eliminating standardized jobs."[6] We know that we are creating a bevy of workers who will need to expect the unexpected, understand the inexplicable, and comprehend technologies that have not yet been invented. Yet the very corporations who will require this of workers want schools to use the same cookie cutter for all students.

What is next? A further stress on the system? Will there be standards for empathy, cooperation, creativity, and joy?

Frederick Douglass has said that it is easier to build strong children than it is to fix broken men. If we cannot provide the former we will need a whole new set of standards to provide the latter.

CHAPTER FOUR

THE GOOD, THE BAD, AND THE UGLY

There are many factors within an educational setting that make it unlike a corporate environment. The politics take on a different hue when no one can be dismissed from the ranks. The blueprints represent the changing faces of a student population that cannot be predicted or controlled. The debris from a changeable society gathers in the entryways of a school and cannot be swept away; it must be allowed in and contended with. This chapter examines those factors typically not faced in a large-scale manner, if at all, within the corporate structure.

SAFETY FIRST

"I just want them to stop." It was a phrase I heard over and over again, while as a principal, from teary-eyed student victims. As part of a tolerance education program, the police–school liaison officer and I worked for two years with students in small groups for twenty minutes a day. Even in that short amount of time, students expressed an amazing capacity to share the hurt, embarrassment, and anger that they had felt because of the overt and covert rejection from their peers. Students consistently shared feelings of inadequacy based on their families' financial status, their intelligence levels, athletic abilities, and cultural backgrounds. Students who feel unworthy in their school environments cannot feel completely safe in those environments. Abraham Maslow's hierarchy of needs places feelings of safety near those of basic needs such as food and shelter. The Dimensions of Learning Model[1] maintains that before students are able to acquire and integrate knowledge, they need to feel comfortable and safe within their learning environments. The Tribes curriculum[2], widely used across the United States, is based on the belief that students must feel like equal members of a shared community before real learning will take place.

TO PROTECT AND SERVE

School business models are mired in policies and procedures that look good on paper. Real students, meanwhile, take that paper and fold it into an airplane to send sailing across the classroom. Policy makers would have us believe that the laws are enough to eliminate the fear factor and protect students.

But the laws only work some of the time for some of the students. The laws designed to protect the rights of handicapped students, for example, can contribute to a negative school climate for others. Consider the case of 14-year-old Joey, labeled "emotionally disturbed" in his school setting. Joey was an eighth grader when I met him. He struggled with impulse control and often called others names, started fights with them, and made inappropriate sexual comments during class. Even when in the small group setting of his special education classroom, Joey had difficulty keeping hands to himself and he frequently touched other students as he walked by their desks. Joey, who was big for his age, wasn't well liked by others and they often teased him by calling him "Lurch" to make him angry. In one such fit of anger, Joey stood up in the cafeteria one day, shoving his tray laden with food at another student while screaming, "I'm going to kill you," followed by a string of expletives. A teacher quickly intervened, leading Joey to the office, while another teacher helped to clean up and calm the students most affected by the tide of Joey's anger.

There are no Joey's in the policy makers' world. With a flick of their fingers, they wave him away, pronouncing him behaviorally unsuitable for the school environment. The politicians disagree, claiming that his school already knew of his behavioral difficulties and were remediating them through his special education program. Furthermore, public law guarantees Joey the right to an education in spite of his behavior. The bottom line is this: while Joey could be educated at an off-site facility at the expense of his school district, he could not be expelled from school entirely. Under current law, students with any special educational status receive the rights associated with disabilities and cannot be discriminated against.

All of this is fine for Joey. Many would hold that beyond that, it is wholly appropriate that he be given every possible opportunity to have his disability remediated. However, what about the other three hundred plus students who saw Joey's display of anger? In a world where school violence is always on the minds of staff and students, will anyone want to share Joey's lunch table? His classroom? His hallways? Until we can standardize Joey and assure that his behavioral deviations will fall within a safe and comfortable norm, we cannot presume to run our schools with the manufactured efficiency of the corporate model.

BUT THEY GET THEIR SUMMERS OFF

Students are not the only public within a school who need to feel safe in order to maximize the effectiveness of curriculum. School staff, too, have suffered the ill effects of increasing school violence. According to the National School Safety Center, which keeps statistics on school violence for the federal government, twenty-nine school staff members—teachers, administrators, custodians, nurses, school police officers—have died violently at work since 1992.

Teacher Dave Sanders was among the thirteen victims of two student gunmen, who killed themselves, in the 1999

Columbine High School shootings in Colorado. In Lake Worth, Florida, teacher Barry Grunow was shot in the head by a student he had sent home earlier on the last day of school in 2000. While assaults continue to be a leading work-related concern for teachers, instances of life-threatening violence are on the rise. In recognition of this the National Education Association (NEA), the nation's largest teachers' union, announced in its September, 2001, newsletter that a $150,000 benefit would be offered for the families of union members slain on the job at school.[3]

Very few people outside of the field of education, and sometimes even those in the educational ranks, give teachers the respect they deserve. If given only for the courage that it takes to teach, respect is still due. It takes courage to stand in front of thirty sets of critical eyes, knowing that for some your voice isn't right, for others your sense of style is all wrong, and that still others hate you simply because they hate math. It takes courage to know that Lupe has an eating disorder, Gerald has a chronic mental illness, and Jamal's father just went to jail . . . and to strive to teach them anyway. It takes courage to know that on any given day, 7 percent of the students encountered are carrying a weapon[4], 54 percent have tried mind-altering substances[5], and that 29 percent are living with at least one unmet basic need.[6] Students must be resilient to survive and thrive. So must teachers. And resiliency must be respected.

In May 2000, CNN did a report on a survey conducted by Scholastics, Inc., and the Council of Chief State School Officers. The survey asked 400 winners of national and state Teacher of the Year awards for solutions to America's growing teacher shortage. Eight out of ten respondents cited the need for more competitive pay and better benefits . . . and an equal number wrote about a need for greater levels of respect from school administrators, legislators, and society at large. Teachers spoke of the political spotlight created by the standards and assessment movement. They spoke about inadequate supplies and technologies that prohibited them from doing their professional best. They spoke of the fact that students themselves see teaching as a disrespected position . . . if not for the behaviors in the classroom but for the obviousness of the low pay of teachers.

Small wonder that high school students don't esteem teaching as a profession when they are already driving better cars than their third-hour history teacher.[7]

LOOK FOR THE UNION LABEL

It was the best of times, it was the worst of times. The Cleavers met the Partridge Family. Sets of values shared, denied, exchanged, and challenged. And the world would never be the same. Unionism, like other manifestos of social growth, decline and change has impacted public school education.

The Sixties. Free speech. Free love. Burning bras. And the rigid men in the straight-backed chairs were challenged. Crisp white shirts met tie-dye. The first brick in the wall that Pink Floyd would later make famous. "We don't need no education," no longer the cry of the simple, but instead, the song of the masses.

It was a time to challenge the infastructure ... to examine the strongholds of society. It was a time of hope to help the little man, to right the wrongs, and to build the bridges that would unite the world. The time for communal bonding together in a common cause. The time when teachers' unions sprang up as educators en masse lost the easy respect that had been theirs by virtue of position.

The goal of the first teachers' union was to protect an endeavor that had become shaky seemingly overnight. The opinionated became public education's number one enemy and quality professionals were rousted from classrooms because their rhetoric did not match the perceived common good. Educational tables turned with the tide and teachers were asked to do more for less. Teaching became the profession best known for substandard wages and precarious job security. As with many of the blue collar unions before and since, the National Education Association did not root itself in a political agenda, but a practical one ... that is, providing the ability to have a decent standard of living and a reasonable level of job security to those entrusted with the task of educating children.

Some might argue that it was the fatal flaw. That the very act of tying respect to a contract only showed teachers to be capitalists who would shoot themselves in the foot to protect their own best interests. The naysayers would later label it the beginning of the end for public schools. In an address to the Economic Freedom forum of the Center for National Policy, Stefan Gleason of the National Right to Work Legal Defense Foundation, Inc., held that the basic philosophy of unionism is the protection of the lowest performer, thus bringing standards of excellence to the lowest common denominator.

Others, however, were poised to recognize the union as a necessary evil in a world that was extending the ends of the bell curve at a rate faster than the pre-established norms could keep up. They would see it as a sad necessity in a world that had abandoned its morals for its freedom. Certainly, many of the educators who were part of the movement viewed their unionization as the only viable means to maintain a "free and appropriate public education for all."

Consider the times. The majority of educators prior to 1961 were female. In 1962, women accounted for 19 percent of union memberships.[8] Much of this unionism could be attributed to the unionism of teachers. In addition, from 1970 to the present, the number of currently divorced adults in the United States has quadrupled.[9] With few laws to protect the rights of single parents and more educators bearing the sole responsibility of supporting a household, the need for steady, protected income became less of a political battle cry and more of a societal necessity.

The union movement was not rooted in public education and had actually been started years before. In fact, when the Federation of Organized Trades and Labor Unions gathered in convention in 1881, Thomas Edison had two years earlier invented the electric light, and the first telephone conversation had taken place just five years before. It became part of the constitution of the Federation of Organized Trades to secure adequate working conditions and tolerable lengths of workdays for the many members of the more localized trade guilds that had already been created.

But what of the impact for the public school and big business analogy? First, picketing educators, although fighting for undeniable needs, did set themselves up to be compared with long lines of blue collar workers. The image of Jimmy Hoffa sleeping with the fishes did little to soothe the public perception of education. In an extreme and unfair view, teachers became just another school of piranha hoping for a chunk of taxpayer flesh to satisfy a hunger that seemed to grow evermore expansive as the public trust diminished. Which came first, the perception or the union? became the question that many in the field of public education still grapple with today.

At some point, the stresses of the past become history and the world breathes one last irritated sigh and demands that we all move on. The last five years of public education have shown a remarkable downslide for the teachers' union in the support of new teachers entering the field. While ingenue teachers are grateful to have the feeling of support and the assurance of a cost of living wage, they are overwhelmingly disengaged from the workings of the union.

The reasons behind this are many. First, the agenda of the NEA has become a very political one. *School Reform News* reports that in 1997 the NEA gave 99 percent of its Political Action Committee (PAC) funds to Democratic candidates although only 42 percent of teachers identify themselves as Democrats.[10] Nearly 80 percent of the dues collected from teachers across the United States goes toward backing political candidates, supporting or denigrating laws that affect public education, and undermining or valuing other parts of a political agenda which has little, if anything, to do with the act of teaching. Yet, overwhelmingly, today's teachers are heard to say that they did not go into the field of education to support a political agenda.

Including unionism in a chapter that focuses on the good, the bad, and the ugly affecting public education is neither a criticism nor a compliment to the effects that the NEA and the AFT have had on education. Necessity has long been the mother of educational invention. Instead, the inclusion of the ideas presented is a call to action and to a new professionalism. It is a prompt for educators everywhere to involve themselves in making their unions professional service organizations focus less on politics and more on the needs of children.

THE RAINBOW CONNECTION

Schools are natural models of diversity. The students who wheel, who walk, and who crawl down the corridors of their school represent a multitude of races, religions, sexual preferences, and financial statuses. They speak with their voices, their hands, their keyboards, and with artificial communication systems. Sometimes, they never speak at all. Some students serve as valedictorians and graduate with the highest of honors. Some members of their class are proud to have mastered basic toileting on that same graduation day. It is the goal of public education to provide equally appropriate educational experiences for every student served. This cannot be done with the eye on cost controls and standardized learning that both government and corporate powers portend as the salvation for the alleged demise of public education.

Equalization costs money. Schools cannot, should not, and would not deny students access to learning because of the expenses associated with providing individual aides to catheterize them, exercise them, feed them, diaper them, assist them with keeping control, interpret for them, respirate them, or give them necessary medications and injections. Schools hire out a tremendous amount of services from occupational therapists, physical therapists, speech and language clinicians, nurses, and alternative educational environments in order to give all within the walls of the school the benefit of a quality curriculum. Many schools provide postsecondary options for students in order to keep them motivated and challenged as they learn.

Not only is equalization costly, it is unpredictable. We are living in an increasingly transient society. Schools cannot deny enrollment to any pupils simply because they are "full," or because they lack the budget monies to educate that student appropriately. During one of my years as a principal, we often joked with worry in our eyes about "taking the billboard encouraging sixth-grade enrollment down." Students were enrolling, midyear, at an alarming rate, especially in sixth grade, where class sizes were already up to thirty in most classes. Teachers didn't have any more desks, any more texts, or any more chairs. There was no additional budget money for staff and the money used to purchase equipment and textbooks for the overflow of students took precious curriculum dollars away from the entire student body. Yet there was nothing to do but make each student feel welcome, and hope that, as in the story of the mitten that housed all the animals of the forest until it burst at its seams, that our educational structure would stay intact for one more day.

TO THE PARENT OR GUARDIAN OF

"Who do you live with?"

Seven-year-old Mikey smiled. "My Gramma Pauline."

"I see you're smiling. Your grandma must make you happy."

A vigorous nod.

"Do you live with a mommy or a daddy, too?"

Suddenly Mikey looked sad. His voice as quiet and his eyes were downcast. "Sometimes Daddy. But mostly Gramma. They had a fight about the dishwasher and my mommy left the house mad."

"I see. That must make you sad."

Another nod.

"Was that just a little while ago?"

A small shrug. "When I was just a little kid." He straightened his shoulders and peeked out from beneath his shaggy blonde bangs. He sighed, "Way back in kindergarten."

I have a theory. Teachers who tire of the classroom would make excellent telemarketers. One of the first things a new teacher learns is the basics of political correctness in "cold-calling" a student's home. First, it is important to not use any last names. Even those on the enrollment card may have changed. It is generally safe to say, "Could I speak to Billy's mother, please?"

Teachers always hope that Billy's mother is at home. If she is not, a whole new set of complications immediately arises. For example, if Billy's mother isn't married to the man who answered the phone, or if he is not legally entitled to hear any school data about Billy, the teacher must refrain from comment and simply ask that Billy's mother call. This usually offends the person on the other end of the phone, as well as offending Billy's mom. Offending the people closest to Billy is not the best way to garner their support.

Teachers always wonder, too, about the etiquette of which parent to call, especially in cases of joint custody, for a child with divorced parents. Do they call the parent with primary physical placement? Both parents? If they call the wrong parent, could they be sued? Can Mikey's grandma actually, legally, learn from his teacher that he is struggling with his spelling or that he is out of medication?

Teachers learn to be civil, too, in spite of the reactions they sometimes receive over the phone. I once had a mother tell me the schedule of her monthly menstrual cycle so that I would make note of it and not bother her on days that she was experiencing PMS.

And teachers must believe in the message they are sending. Often, the same message needs to be sent time and again and even again before parents will heed it. There is an evolution to the acceptance that our children are not perfect.

THIRTY-THREE'S A CROWD

Overcrowding in schools became a "hot topic" in education in 1995, when both the Institute for Urban and Minority Education (IUME) and the Citizen's Commission on Planning for Enrollment Growth did studies on urban school overcrowding in New York City. Like its urban counterparts across the United States, New York City is now facing dramatic overcrowding with a 2002 enrollment figure of over one million students.[11] A statement by the President in August 2000 acknowledges that in the 2000–2001 school year, a record 52 million students enrolled in American schools. The statement relates, "Over the last ten years, our public schools have grown by 6.6 million students, resulting in overcrowded classrooms and strained school facilities."[12]

There are several negative impacts associated with overcrowding. While in some cases overcrowding is positively associated with effective school programs and subsequent school choice, in most instances overcrowding, especially in schools with high poverty levels, has a dire effect on learning and on standardized test performance. Crowded classrooms make concentration difficult for students and limit the amount of time and space that teachers have available for creative teaching methods such as cooperative learning and group work. The likelihood of teacher burnout increases with the amount of time spent in simply keeping classroom order. Overcrowding forces schedule changes that are not always in students' best interests (e.g., eating lunch at 10:30 A.M.), necessitates sharing lockers, creates more violent overcrowded hallways, and lessens instructional time by mandating additional "passing time" in hallways.

Most seriously, though, electives such as art, music, and technology education classes (such as family and consumer education and woodworking) are slashed from school schedules at worst, and placed "on a traveling" cart at best. In either scenario, students are not able to receive the full benefits of instruction in those areas.

MISSING THE POMP AND CIRCUMSTANCE

The importance of a high school education has increased exponentially over the past fifty years. While it was once an asset to entry into the workforce, today is it a minimum requirement for entry into even the most basic tasks within the skilled labor force. A strong focus on providing students with a minimum of technological skills is necessary for schools.

There are several issues surrounding the quagmire of school attendance. Homelessness, transiency, and truancy have a daily (even hourly) impact on student programming and subsequent school completion. Too often, school attendance is brought to the public only by the reporting of dropout rates. It is equally, if not more important, to report high school completion rates. The high school completion rate represents the proportion of 18 to 24 year olds who have completed a high school diploma or equivalent credential, including a General Educational Development (GED) credential. Despite the increased importance of high school education, the high school completion rate has increased only slightly in the last twenty-five years. The current rate of completion is 86 percent of students, a net increase of 3 percent in 28 years. The national goal for high school completion is 90 percent.

Dropout rates, however, are the most common figures reported to the American public. In 1999, 3.8 million young adults were not enrolled in high school programs and had not completed high school. The status dropout rate remains lower for whites than blacks but the gap has consistently narrowed over the last quarter of a century. The dropout rate for Hispanic youth is significantly higher than that of other nationalities within the United States. In 1999, 44.2 percent of Hispanic young adults born outside of the United States were high school dropouts. Although Hispanic youth born in the United States were far less likely to drop out, school completion rates remain lowest for Hispanic students.[13]

School attendance is reflective of family values, societal norms, and socioeconomic pressures. The renewed emphasis on high-stakes testing and twelfth-grade exit assessments required for graduation may diminish students' drives to stay in school. At-risk students become at-risk because they have difficulty succeeding in traditional, assessment-focused models of education. The pressures inherent in a school (not a student) performing well on standardized assessments will have a negative impact on dropout rates and will further segregate learners by increasing enrollment in nontraditional diploma equivalency programs. At worst, students will begin to view schools as detached, aloof, test-taking institutions and they will drop out without ever dropping back in.

JUST WAIT TILL YOUR FATHER
GETS HOME

For some of America's children, this is a long wait. The majority of children in the United States are now growing up in families in which both parents or the only parent works outside of the home. It has now become commonplace in our society for children to take care of themselves for periods of time every day. Recent census data suggests that about 7.2 percent (or 2 million) children between the ages of 5 and 13 spend regular time each day involved in self-care because there is not an adult present in their living environment.[14]

What does this mean for education? There are a number of detrimental impacts from the latchkey child phenomenon. First, students are often not supervised during the hours following school dismissal. There is a high correlation between juvenile delinquency and unsupervised time. Students who are ill-prepared for high degrees of freedom often do not use their time responsibly and tend to build a greater reliance on peers as a result. In many areas, especially large urban areas, the reliance on a group of peers has led to breakdowns in the family and increased gang activities.

This, of course, has the potential for serious, long-range negative effects or children left with too much responsibility for their own care. The shorter-range effects include less focus on homework, less communication between schools and parents, and students who mature more quickly than is developmentally appropriate. In response to these perceived negatives, many schools have contracted on-site child-care, offered afterschool homework sessions, and have made attempts to keep communication strong by offering interactive events for parents, students, and teachers outside of normal school hours.

THIS LITTLE PIGGY WENT
TO NO HOME

The number of homeless children living in the United States is on the rise. Some 5.2 million children under the age of six live well below the poverty line established by the federal government. Not surprisingly, high levels of poverty correlate with three key factors—single parenthood, employment, and degree of high school education. Research opportunities with homeless children are difficult because of the transitory and migratory nature of being homeless. What is known is that the level of chronic illnesses among homeless children is 40 percent higher than that of their peers, especially with regard to asthma, ear infections, and stomach ailments. They have nutritional deficiencies, significantly slower rates of development cognitively, socially, emotionally, and physically, and more frequent behavior difficulties. About a fifth of homeless children have emotional difficulties severe enough to warrant professional care but the likelihod of treatment drops as the severity of their mental illness increases.[15] Homeless children are also typically witnesses to high degrees of domestic violence (92 percent of homeless mothers have been abused severely physically or sexually, often by an intimate partner or family member).

The 80 percent of homeless children who attend school are transient and often attend several schools over the course of a year. Twenty percent never attend school at all. It is impossible to have parent communication for homeless children; there are no addresses to send reports, no phones to check on absences, and no means to share any good news with parents.

Such are some of the major dividing lines between the public and private sector. Imagine that three adult members of the same dysfunctional family walk into the human resources department of a large corporation. They each demand placement where they feel they will work best. Human resources personnel would be expected to link them with the appropriate Employee Assistance Programs to counsel their various emotional problems. Each person would need to be equipped with all the trappings of a cubicle, would need to have all the paperwork necessary to work for the corporation explained to them, and would need to be introduced to all the implicit and explicit rules of the company. It would probably be a good idea for the human resources staff to help them get clean clothing, a means to a shower and basic hygiene supplies, and a nutritious meal plan. Employees in other cubicles could quickly become dissatisfied themselves if they have to inhale the pungent aroma of life on the streets.

The above scenario is impractical and costly and is made more so by a great likelihood that the family would simply move on to another corporation soon after their employment training was complete. Impractical and costly? Inconvenient and time consuming? Certainly. But it happens every day in schools all across the United States. Homeless students enroll and are placed in grade levels. They are given desks, materials, textbooks, and other necessary school supplies. They are provided ancillary services devoted to health, nutrition, and emotional well being. Often, they are provided new clothing and hygiene items. They are provided with a piece of a classroom teacher's heart . . . and often, they simply move away as quickly as they arrived.

THE HEART OF THE MATTER

There have always been concerns about too much governmental control over a school's mission. In 1903, Dewey stated, "The dictation of the subject matter to be taught and the methods to be used in teaching, mean nothing more or less than the deliberate restriction of intelligence, the imprisoning of the spirit."[16] Single parent homes. Latchkey children. Teen parents. Children living on the streets. Non-English-speaking learners. Poverty levels. Schools are reflections of society as a whole. None of the issues cited in this chapter can be cured by raising the standards, increasing professionalism, or requiring exit exams. When we speak of public school failure, we must take a hard look at the failures in the greater American society and seek solutions that reflect a comprehensive effort on behalf of all people. It is time to start giving schools the autonomy to enact missions that reflect a concern for not just academic standards, but character standards. It is time to allow curriculum to reflect the creativity and talents of the teacher delivering it. It is time to actively encourage environments that care less about test scores and more about children.

CHAPTER FIVE

HOW DO I TEST THEE?

Student assessment plays a colossal role in the political agendas of government leaders and educational policy makers. It is often the cause for disdain from the media, panic from parents, and stress for students. This chapter examines the natural dissonance that occurs as educators attempt to instruct using a broad and appropriate curriculum, infuse content specific standards, and ultimately feel forced to "teach to the test."

ON THE ROAD AGAIN

Imagine having to take your driving test every year. Do you remember all those rules of the road that you learned the first time around? Would your livelihood depend on passing the test? Do you suppose employers would start to offer tutorials to keep their employees on the road?

You might protest. Nothing has changed, you might say. The rules of the road are the same today as they were twenty years ago. There is no reason to test again and again and again. But surely you've changed automobiles at least once. Have you read the new owner's manual? Car manufacturers are always updating their standards and creating safer and more reliable products. Shouldn't consumers be expected to be current with regard to the influx of information that is available regarding their vehicle? After all, if we want to test children every year in school on the basic knowledge that they are receiving, just to make sure that they are actually receiving it, doesn't it make sense that we would expect the same sort of accountability for adults?

Let's extend the analogy even further and make the car manufacturers themselves wholly responsible for the process of educating consumers. If Mrs. Jones on Maple Street doesn't want to learn about her engine, those automobile moguls will simply have to find a way to make her want to learn or risk high-cost sanctions invoked for failing to educate American drivers.

Why stop with the auto industry? Shouldn't the owners of washing machines, blow dryers, refrigerators, and handguns have to take a test each year, too? It isn't enough to be provided with safety and product information . . . that information must be embraced and internalized. The common good is at stake!

Sounds, ridiculous, doesn't it? But it is exactly the mentality that is driving the high-stakes testing phenomenon that is sweeping American public schools. The public outcry for accountable students masks an even larger demand that teachers be accountable for delivering a common curriculum. As in the case with poor old Mrs. O'Leary and her cow, the public wants someone to blame for the societal ills it experiences.

What policy makers fail to define is the real relationship between testing and knowledge. After all, how many car accidents have been caused by people who aced the written part of their driving test? Doesn't the real measure of on-the-road knowledge lie in performance? The only way to improve performance is to practice. No one hands the keys to the family car to a sixteen year old and just says "Drive." Not even when that sixteen year old could be driving to his eighth-grade classroom to take his standardized test for the ninth time.

HOW DO YOU LIKE YOUR STAKES?

It used to be that the eternal question was "which came first, the chicken or the egg?" Our modern results-driven society has formed a new answer to this query. It seems the reply en masse is a chorus of "who cares as long as we have an egg." Today's students take less time to ponder, less time to process, and move more quickly to producing outcomes than ever before. And who can blame them? We watch fast-paced talk shows, short-lived sitcoms, and music videos that shift our visual focus at astounding rates. Americans eat at fast-food restaurants, invented grocery store express lines, toll-booth pass systems that allow quicker transit, and swipe and go gas stations, grocery stores, and department stores. The computer has progressed from dinosaur to Internet road runner and the plethora of interactive materials that extend reality and shorten attention spans is common everywhere. Students are raised with the belief that faster must be better.

Then we ask them to go back to the basics. Right-wing educational gurus shake their heads and wonder why we can't just return to the good old days of reading, writing, and arithmetic. Policy makers collect standards in cheery baskets and scatter them down the hallways of schools with carefree abandon. Rigor, students are told, is everything. Failing to learn is learning to fail and the only acceptable demonstration of knowledge is the numerical score on a standardized test. Success is not measured in inches. It is not a snapshot of everyday life but a portrait of once-a-year finery. Learning is a product; not a process. It doesn't matter how the answer is found . . . only that it *is* found . . . and most importantly that it can be memorized and transferred to a surreal pencil and paper assessment.

No wonder students are confused. They are immersed in water already moving as if at a full boil and told to simultaneously swim and learn to swim. They are given less time to learn more information and they are taught fewer strategies for storing and retrieving that information. They live in a society that tells them to live fast, learn fast, and scorn the process for the product. Yet they are tested on how much they have learned and not at the speed at which they have accumulated that knowledge. Which came first? In the long run, the answer will have to be generated by those who created the high-stakes insanity. Right after they wipe the egg off of their faces.

CASTE YOUR CARES AWAY

As more and more public school systems are confronted with the expectation that they administer standardized tests that are inappropriate for large numbers of their students, those who bear the brunt of the test results have begun to do what members of the legal profession have know how to do for years—look for the loopholes.

It sounds rather shady . . . as if hordes of educators are meeting with one another in dark back alleys to exchange test evasion secrets. Never have the letter and the spirit of the law been so in conflict with one another. Never has the letter so often won.

Special education students, for example, can be excluded from testing if there is appropriate justification in their Individual Education Plan. It is tempting to find such justification. After all, those who are not tested cannot skew the results. But what of equal opportunity and least restrictive environment? Special education students are held to the same educational standards when they are in a classroom. Often, modifications in curriculum are made and modifications to testing can be made, too. Test time restrictions can be lifted and test questions can be read aloud to less-able readers with assessment provisions in their educational plans. Perhaps, then, it is better to have students in special education programs. It certainly seems to be the trend. The number of children served by federally funded special education programs has been on the rise since the inception of such programs with the enactment of Public Law 94-142 in 1975. In 1976, approximately 8 percent of a public school's total enrollment was determined to have some level of handicapping condition. In 1999, that figure rose to 13 percent.[1] Between 1977 and 1996, the number of students in special education grew 52 percent while public school enrollment increased by 1 percent.[2] It is my prediction that the pressures of high-stakes testing and the false accountability that such tests purport will serve to segregate learners to an alarming degree. Schools will seek to offer more specialized programs to more students and the bell curve will start to flatten as a result. The minority of learners will become the majority by default. It was once said that the problem with nonconformists is that they are all so much alike. Schools will no longer need to worry about the nonconformists because there will be so many pigeon-holes available. The true bane of the standardized tests, the nonperformists, will be pushed and prodded toward the end of the bell curve that will allow their test results to be discounted. How long will it be before the cry of "Johnny Can't Read" is replaced with "Johnny Can't Communicate"? How long before the pendulum will start to push the students back to a common ground? How long before the line on the bell-shaped curve becomes so flat that the pulse of education can no longer be detected?

GENERATION UNXCITED

Politics aside, many school districts historically have not given students standardized tests every year. At a minimum, however, most students across the United States have been tested every four academic years, in the fourth and eighth grades and then as juniors in high school as part of a graduation requirement. Schools begin the testing process in the junior year of high school so that students who have failed to beat the test the first time around can be given additional opportunities to retake the exam and graduate with their peers.

There are several factors that inhibit the successful testing of students at these age levels and none of them have to do with the curriculum that is being delivered in the classroom. First, consider brain development. Studies show that children experience more rapid brain growth between birth and 10 years of age, with the preschool years being the most critical times of brain development.[3] In the subsequent years, students may grow and change physically, but do not integrate new knowledge as rapidly. Often, especially during the teen years, these less academic periods are devoted to learning communication and social skills. Why then, do test makers and policy makers alike want schools to test during the years of less-efficient learning?

Could it possibly be because scores are more adversely affected and thus more tutorial supplemental materials are sold? Could it be because lower scores allow politicians to place a heavy hand in an iron fist and mandate a tougher, more rigorous curriculum? Could it be because the people who write the standards fear having to sell hamburgers if an acceptable set of standards is ever defined?

Second, consider what is known about adolescents. When high-stakes testing gets into the ring with hormones, it is sure to be knocked out of the match. If the steady chatter of teens on the telephone, in the mall, and involved in all of the extracurricular activities that are offered within a school don't sap the strength of the standards, then the adolescent angst, dedication to caffeine and junk food, and the whirl of personalities being tried on and changed on a whim will surely drain the power from the politicians' postulates of excellence. In short, it is impractical to place high-stakes outcomes on children who get furtive tattoos, daydream of being the first to pierce their left eyebrows, and still sleep with teddy bears. Minds that are learning to acclimate to the adult world are still minds that are learning. It is too easy to forget that our students are becoming people and not statistics.

Students are at their most vulnerable points of social development at the time when high-stakes testing means the most. President George W. Bush's plan to assess students each year between third and eighth grade purports to use standardized test measures on students for a period of six years (grades three through eight) during which research clearly demonstrates that social development and interaction is far more significant to youth. Chapter Five will examine this idea in greater detail.

Educators, especially at the middle level, have known for years that all information must pass through the social strainer before it can be adopted as acceptable. Teaching methods such as small group work, cooperative learning, think-pair-share, and the five-step writing process maximize the academic curriculum for social learners. Unfortunately, standardized testing does not follow suit. During a standardized test, students work in isolation from one another on a nonintegrated body of knowledge. Moreover, given the many pressures at both parental and at school-based levels, students are often being asked to draw upon pre-existing knowledge under conditions of trepidation and tension. Testing the afraid until they become the ashamed is a moral outrage in light of what we know about how children learn best.

Third, the amount of adult stresses that older teens experience continues to rise. In a study of more than 8,000 high school students and people in their early twenties, close to two-thirds of subjects polled reported feeling stressed at least once a week. Additionally, a full one-third of U.S. teens say they feel stressed out on a daily basis. Researchers found that American teens reported feeling anxious and aggressive on a somewhat regular basis. In the month before the survey was taken, participants said they were more likely to say that they felt like hitting someone, destroying something, or picking fights with other students.[4]

In addition to the stresses caused by the increasing societal pressures (drug use, gang activity, school violence, AIDS, terrorism, and increasing socioeconomic inequities), teens often take on adult responsibilities in their homes and communities. Approximately one-third of all teenagers in the United States were employed in 1998. In a mirror of society-at-large, the average incomes of students from low-income families were significantly lower than those of their peers who did not have low-income status.[5] In order to maximize work experiences for all youth, schools offer many programs that allow teens to access the world of work quickly and with appropriate school supervision. Such programs are designed to assist businesses in obtaining qualified graduates and to enable schools to remain on the cutting edge of what is expected in the "real world." Unfortunately, as the number of curricular standards gets higher and higher, many high schools are being forced to cut programs, including youth employment programs, in order to add more required classes to their school schedules. Testing plays a significant role in this unfortunate phenomenon. The junior year of high school has traditionally been a time of challenging classes. The typical junior year curriculum is designed to give students an added edge on college entrance. Students learn and apply knowledge within a fairly quick "turn around" time. However, college entrance exams, such as the SATs, are general knowledge exams.

They ask students to perform tasks from a generalized group of data, using learning strategies as well as a large amount of prior knowledge. Students must be able to retrieve information that has been educationally stockpiled for many years. On the other hand, the standardized tests that students are given are more closely linked to explicit curricular standards. A student who takes such a standardized test in his junior year may need to recall specific information learned as an eighth or ninth grader. If distinct pockets of information cannot be recalled for the assessment, scores will fall into unacceptable ranges. In response, many schools are pressured to add content specific classes to the repertoire of expectations that already exist. For example, if students are expected to have knowledge about the Civil Rights Movement and they test in their junior year, and they take Modern History as freshmen, they may have forgotten key elements that relate directly to the standards. Thus, either additional history classes need to be added in the first semester of the junior year, or classes that are less visible on the state exams need to be reshuffled and replaced with more standard-specific course work. In either scenario, a tighter schedule always means less flexibility to do diversified programs such as school-to-work. Cutbacks in the ability to provide school-to-work experiences also create greater chasms for low-income youth who are denied the opportunities to learn appropriate job skills.

Finally, we are living in a time when being disenfranchised is almost a cultural expectation among adolescents and teens. Most youth fall somewhere along a continuum of total apathy and responsible leadership. The continuum can best be divided into three stages: apathy, awareness, and responsibility. Unfortunately, for a large majority of youth, apathy becomes the standard rather than the catalyst for growth. The causes of detachment and apathy for youth are difficult to determine. In an article on youth leadership, David Grummon[6] cites the lingering legacy of Generation X, who made not caring "cool" and coined phrases such as "whatever" into a consciousness that continues to invade the youth culture of today. As mentioned in Chapter Two of this book, Grummon also cites propensity for our culture to see youth as a target market group instead of as future leaders as a cause of teen detachment. Because teens are among the hottest demographic groups for advertising, they receive a flood of media messages prescribing the "best" way to dress, act, and live. When youth become passive receptors of ideas, they learn that they are not expected to think for themselves.

The term *detached youth* refers to young people ages 16 to 19 who are neither enrolled in school nor working; 1996 statistics show that 9 percent of youth could fall under the classification of "detached." The number is higher for women and minorities.[7] It is critical to note that detachment not only begets detachment, it also has a strong correlation to poverty levels. These income levels, in turn, continue the cycle by impacting teen pregnancy rates, school dropout rates, school attendance rates, and, subsequently, standardized test scores. While the teens "not served" by public schools cannot have a directly negative impact on test results, we are already immersed in providing services to the generation of children born of "detached" parents. It is not a cycle that can or will correct itself through the efforts of public education alone and it is inappropriate that our public schools alone bear the brunt of the media's disdain for test scores that are struggling to stay in or reach a satisfactory range.

A BRAIN, A HEART, THE NERVE

The at-risk students that I teach struggle with self-concept. I have a large poster in my classroom depicting Gardner's[8] seven types of intelligence. I frequently remind my students that there is more to life than academia. I stress the importance of musical and kinesthetic intelligences. I tell them all how interpersonally intelligent and intuitive they are. I tell them what a gift those skills are to the workplace. I encourage Andreas in his art and Elizabeth in her singing. It is my goal to help my students feel that they are capable and intelligent not only because it is vital to have self-confidence to succeed in life, but because they are. Students become at-risk learners for a variety of reasons. However, the most prominent reason is that they are not traditional learners. They are the square pegs in the round holes of academia.

It is not that they cannot or will not learn information; they simply need it provided through alternate channels.

We had two full days of standardized testing at our school this year. It made my students visibly concerned, tired, and depressed. One of the girls in my classroom summed it up most succinctly. As she handed me her test booklet, she was near tears. In her frustration, she asked, "So, when I fail this test like I know I will . . . are you going to write to them and tell them that I'm smart?"

In recent years, technological and scientific advances have allowed for an increasingly in-depth study of the brain. Several of the learning principles associated with the brain are in direct conflict with the objectives of standardized tests.[9] First, the brain is a social brain. Learning, therefore, is profoundly influenced by the nature of the social relationships within which people find themselves. Standardized testing is an artificial and asocial phenomenon.

The search for meaning occurs through "patterning." Effective education must give learners an opportunity to formulate their own patterns of understanding. Paper and pencil assessments most often provide a series of isolated skills that vary not only page by page but subsection by subsection. Tests are usually administered to fit into a time frame of school bells and class schedules with little regard for even a modicum of sequencing of skills to be tested. Emotions are critical to patterning. An appropriate emotional climate is indispensable to a sound education. An unnatural and stress-filled environment is common to most classrooms administering standardized tests.

Learning involves both conscious and unconscious processes. Much of learning is unconscious in that sensory input is processed below the level of awareness. This means that learning may not occur during a class but may occur hours, weeks, or months later. Perhaps we should have students carry their tests with them and fill them in over the course of a school year and during the summer months. Have you ever noticed how the phenomenon of déjà vu that occurs around learning something new? For instance, when a new word is added to a vocabulary, it suddenly seems as if that word is everywhere, in text and in dialogue. It is because our consciousness is suddenly awakened to new learning. Children experience this circumstance repeatedly in the process of learning and storing new information.

Complex learning is enhanced by challenge and inhibited by threat. The brain learns optimally when it is appropriately challenged in an environment that encourages risk taking. However, the mind "downshifts" under perceived threat. The essential element of perceived threat is a feeling of helplessness and fatigue. In surreal situations, we hand students a paper and pencil assessment that will require them to exhibit knowledge in disconnected "sound bites." After spending our instructional time encouraging them to ask questions and use resources to find answers, we tell them they may not. Classrooms that are typically alive with movement and voice become silent and still. Can we be creating anything other than helplessness and fatigue?

LEADING HORSES TO WATER

In 1976, the Association of Childhood Education International (ACEI) issued a position paper calling for a moratorium on standardized testing in the early years of school. Although pressure to test continued in the late 1970s, there was also vigorous debate about the negative effects of testing. Support for authentic forms of assessment rooted in close observation and systematic documentation of children's learning became more common.[10,11] With the publication of *A Nation at Risk*[12], the pendulum once again began to swing toward a standardized assessment mentality.

Standardized testing is problematic for students of all ages but is particularly questionable in the primary grades. In these years, a child's growth is most uneven and in large measure is idiosyncratic. The skills needed for success in school are in their most fluid stages and the implication of failure on a standardized measure are most devastating. Testing in the early years has an effect on self-esteem, serves to distort curriculum, teaching, and learning and actually results in a lowering of expectations. The results of testing for students in kindergarten and the primary grades are deleterious, particularly for poor and minority children.[13] An article in *Working Mother* summed it up as follows, "It's the drip, drip, drip of daily experiences that affect a child's development."[14] So what do we hope to accomplish under umbrellas of standardized assessments?

In 2002 the National Council for the Social Studies (NCSS) joined with the National Council of Teachers of English, the International Reading Association, and the American Educational Research Association in supporting long-term authentic assessment and opposing high-stakes standardized assessment. A glimpse into the position statement offered by the NCSS offers insight into the reason for their opposition to high-stakes testing.

> Whereas high stakes standardized tests represent a powerful intrusion into American's classrooms, often taking up as must as 30% of teacher time . . .
>
> Whereas these tests measure, for the most part, parental income and race, and are therefore instruments that build racism and anti-working class sentiment . . .
>
> Whereas these tests deepen the segregation of children within and between school systems . . .
>
> Whereas these tests create an atmosphere that puts students against students and teachers against teachers and school systems against school systems in a mad scramble for financial rewards and to avoid financial retribution . . .
>
> Whereas the tests foment an atmosphere of greed, fear, and hysteria, none of which contributes to learning . . .
>
> Whereas the tests become commodities for opportunities whose interests are profits, not the best interests of children . . .[15]

Paul Houston, the executive director of the American Association of School Administrators holds that the inherent inequities that result from standardized tests create a direct clash with the American system of values. The tests are a single indicator that can effectively change the direction of a child's life. Tests certainly change teacher and parent perceptions. Test results change students' perceptions of themselves. Educational environments are limited or expanded based on the perceptions created by an isolated paper and pencil occurrence. Houston says, "Making kids perform like trained seals at the demand of politicians might be entertaining, but it is not good education. Using a single test to determine a child's future is a lousy way to create educational improvement. It is even a worse way to educate an American."[16]

THE FEAR FACTOR

America's public schools have responded to the pressures of high stakes in a variety of ways. Curricula have changed, standards have become more prominent and are more professed in the public arena, and classroom teaching and learning has been altered to better enable children to become good test takers. All of these things have been done at a cost. The primary cost is the creativity of classroom teachers and a stifling of the diversity within schools.

But there is another cost to test preparation. Many schools find themselves spending tens of thousands of dollars on test-preparation materials. In fact, the test prep industry has become worth about $2.5 billion in recent years. Companies like Kaplan, Sylvan Learning, TestU, and Princeton Review are among several of their ilk. In the three years since The Princeton Review created its grade-school division, it has signed contracts with schools in twenty-five states. The company now sells more than 500 guidebooks to state exams and sprinkles test-taking tips throughout more than 36 textbooks published by McGraw-Hill. In the summer of 2000, it launched Homework.com, an online bank of more than 120,000 practice questions to help teachers pinpoint their students' strengths and weak spots. The firm's latest offering is a $1950 primer for parents on test-taking skills that, among other things, instructs them to serve an extra large breakfast on test day.[17]

Executives at TestU have gone a step further than most companies in zeroing in on the students and schools they seek to serve. The Internet-based company has so far developed state-specific preparation programs only in those states with exit exams that students must pass to graduate. "It is our mission to focus on those states where the pain is greatest," said Edmundo Gonzalez, a vice president of the New York City–based company, which has preparation programs for state tests in Florida, Massachusetts, New York, and Texas. "We focus on places where there's risk both to the administrators and the students." In creating their professional-development seminars and materials, officials at Kaplan say they have also honed their programs to serve those schools and districts where the need is the greatest, reaching out specifically to educators in schools—particularly those in urban areas—with large number of students who do not do well on state tests.[18]

High-stakes testing and all of its subsidiary components beget a system of exploitation. Schools are exploited first by the press and responsively by alleged test-taking panaceas such as those offered in the newest megamarket of test preparation materials. The greatest exploitation, however, comes not to a school's publicity or its pocketbook, although both of these are noteworthy. The greatest exploitation is our nation's children— those who are placed on pedestals for high test achievement and those who are placed in programs because they did not achieve. Schools are engaged in intellectual and emotional combat, victimized by their own fear of public humiliation and government sanctions. Public schools across America must take a unified stand against the ills of standardized testing. Intimidation has produced artificial education. The fear must stop so that real learning, once again, may start.

CHAPTER SIX

A BETTER MOUSETRAP

This chapter examines the role that nontraditional educational environments play in tandem with traditional public education. School choice, vouchers, charters, and for-profit edventures are examined in terms of the impact felt by the educational arena as a whole.

ROUND AND AROUND AND AROUND SHE GOES

In every teachers' lounge of every school that I've ever worked in, I've heard the phrase "Just tell me what to do and I'll do it," at least once. When it is uttered, heads around the table invariably nod in agreement. Many teachers were model students. They are good at both understanding and following a prescribed set of directions. They excel at performing curricular tasks according to the guidelines suggested by their teachers' manuals. They enjoy tasks with definitive endings and feel deep satisfaction in having successfully completed a wide array of instructional "objectives." It should be easy, then, to mandate a set of educational standards that can be assessed on a national scale.

A mousetrap is a mousetrap but not all mousetraps are alike. The end product is measurable, of course, but the process to achieving that outcome can vary greatly. So it is with education. Theoretically, each teacher can build her own mousetrap so long as students reach the ultimate goal of passing a standardized test. Some may teach directly to the test while others may employ a wide variety of test preparation materials to help their students become conversant with testing materials. Still others may simply close their classroom doors and teach as they always have, hoping that there is enough content within that instruction to reach the goal.

It sounds simple; however, for many of the reasons described in Chapter Four, the process of educating students is NOT simple. It is daunting and the importance of a single score on a single measure inspires a good deal of fear in many schools. Far more frightening, though, is the subtle implication behind the goal: that the passing of a standardized test has become THE goal of a well-rounded education. Educators who are poised to be told "what to do" suddenly have lists and rubrics. They have accountability they can identify and adhere to. They have an alleged formula for professional success.

The protest reaches my fingertips as I type the words. But what about creativity? Self-definition? Personalization? The late U.S. Senator Paul Wellstone commented, "The best teachers just hate being in a testing straightjacket. High-stakes testing is channeling teaching to the kind of rote memorization drill that isn't education."[1] The routinized expectations inherent in a national assessment do seem to favor a standardized process of not only curriculum but of curriculum delivery. However, it is the aforementioned traits that are the inspiration behind movements such as school choice, charter schools, magnet schools, and school vouchers.

THE GREAT RACE

Picture a long journey. It is late August and you must drive from New York to California. There are several vehicles at your disposal, ranging from a jalopy in need of repairs to a mid-sized sedan to a fully loaded convertible to a luxurious stretch limousine complete with wet bar and television. As an average American, you have a certain amount of money to spend on the transportation for your trip. You are told that the sedan, which is adequately comfortable, relatively safe, and fairly reliable is free. The convertible comes at a cost and the limousine requires you to take out a loan. You've really not even considered the jalopy.

What would be the best mode of transportation? Your response would depend largely on your pocketbook and your feelings of security. Would that response change if you were given additional transportation funds to be put toward the convertible or the limousine?

Consider, too, how the vehicles are being advertised. Adequately comfortable, relatively safe, and fairly reliable? Fully-loaded? Luxurious? It would seem silly to take the sedan if the limo could be subsidized. One need not even consider looking under the hood to make a decision. Fiscal prudence may still dictate the convertible but the simple act of being offered a monetary voucher has taken the sedan out of consideration.

In an article on the issues of school choice, John Merrifield[2] speaks not about which vehicle will be driven but the effects of an educational market in which private schools are subsidized by taxpayer funds. He says, "Departures [from public schools] would occur disproportionately in families willing to supplement the taxpayer funds with their own funds and in families most actively involved in their child's education—the students and the parents whose support and involvement the public schools can least afford to lose. Education outcomes may improve for society as a whole, but an accelerated decline of public schools could hurt low-income families forced to choose between those schools and the cheapest private schools."

He makes a good point. There is a wide body of research citing the potential prejudicial practices occurring in conjunction with voucher programs, charter schools, and expanded school choice options. Moreover, it has yet to be proven that private is really better. In the long drive of education, if one fails to look under the hood, the potential for breakdown is far greater. Private school choices and vouchers may at first appear to be the panacea that will soothe the hardships experienced by students in struggling public schools. An expansion of choice and a provision for funding that choice may seem a gift to a parent who is concerned about their child's safety, welfare, or perceived educational attainment. The argument for private school choice, however, is built on the premise that private schools are more efficient than their public school counterparts.

The widespread and growing appeal of public/private schools choice can be attributed to several key factors. First, on average, private school students outperform their public school peers in terms of standardized test scores, graduation rates, and the probability of attending college.[3] The Condition of Education[4] report indicates that there are some solid reasons behind the private schools' academic achievements and give evidence that other contrasts between the two environments show less diversity in private schools.

• Public schools tend to have more racially and ethnically diverse student populations

• Public schools have more students with Limited English Proficiency

• Personal problems that interfere with learning are more of a problem in public schools

• Private schools have fewer minority teachers and principals

• More public school teachers have achieved advanced educational degrees than private school teachers

• Public schools tend to have larger enrollments and greater class sizes

• Private school principals report having more influence over curriculum than do public school administrators

• Private school teachers report having more autonomy in the classroom

• Exposure to crime or threats is more common in public schools

• Private school teachers share a greater sense of community within their schools

• Public school teachers are more likely to believe that a lack of parental support is a serious problem in their school

Another appeal of school vouchers is that more control over educational decisions is given to parents. When more control is yielded to the consumers of education, those who presumably have the best knowledge of the educational needs and desires of children are allowed to use that knowledge in selecting a school. Since most parents believe that they know what it best for their children, choice and subsequent vouchers become an issue of political correctness.[5]

Politics are definitely on President George W. Bush's mind. In spite of the fact that Congress rejected private-school vouchers in 2001, Bush again proposed such vouchers in his 2003 budget. Bush proposes giving tax dollars to families trying to get their children out of struggling public schools. But rather than give families money for private school tuition, Bush is asking for tax credits of up to $2500 per family. This allowance could even be collected by families who don't owe $2500 in taxes provided they spend at least $5000 to send their child from a "failing" public school to a private school. Families could recoup the costs of sending a child to a different public school or home schooling. Covered expenses would include transportation, textbooks, and home computers.[6]

RISKY BIG BUSINESS

Tax credits and vouchers run synonymous risks. Given a chance to slip behind the wheel of a convertible, many families will do so, leaving empty sedans in their wake. There are certainly features that make the convertible more appealing. It matters little if the transportation is really the same. In an adolescent culture that values money and social envy, new and different will always triumph over tried and true. Martin Carnoy, professor of education and economics at Stanford University, maintains that "Voucher plans increase inequality without making schools better. Even more significantly, privatization reduces the public effort to improve schooling since it relies on the free market to increase achievement. But the increase never occurs."[7] In addition, Goldhaber refers to a phenomenon of "selection bias" that can occur when there are important unobservable characteristics of students that influence achievement. These characteristics might include student motivation or the educational environment of a student's home.[8] Unreported inequalities in assessment between public and private schools encourage selection bias. While it is statistically proven that academic scores are higher in private schools, the students taking the tests and making the grades started at higher levels in the private schools. Thus, early learning opportunities and parental support contribute positively to school success. Such opportunities are more prevalent in the homes of private school students. This is not to detract from the many parents of public school students who provide similar experiences. However, as the Condition of Education reports, families with annual incomes over $50,000 have the most choice. Higher family incomes facilitate both public and private school choices. Because most private schools charge tuition, only parents with the personal financial resources or financial aid truly have the option of selecting a private school. Similarly, because housing options can influence a family's income, the percentage of parents who reported that their choice of residence was influenced by where their children would go to school also generally increased with family income.[9] Controlling for differences in individuals, families, and school resources, Goldhaber found no significantly statistical effect of private schools on math and reading test scores. Although private school students have higher mean test scores than do public school students, the mean differences between the school sectors can be attributed to differences in the characteristics of students attending those schools rather than the differences in the "teaching capability" of the schools. Essentially, private schools attract students who are from better educated, wealthier families and who enter school with above average standardized test scores.

Academics notwithstanding, opponents of vouchers maintain that they are inherently prejudicial. A few thousand dollars a year will not cover the yearly costs of many private schools. And many students whose parents can make the tuition payments will not be admitted to the schools of their choice. Private schools choose their students and they may reject or expel the most troubled kids who need the most help. It's not surprising that private schools appear to foster achievement in kids; they choose not to deal with failure.[10] An even stronger sentiment by writer Wendy Kaminer says that the trade-off of civil liberties is simply not worth making:

> ...vouchers will not significantly expand civil rights—access to equal education and all that it promises—but they will restrict civil liberties. By directing government funds to parochial schools, vouchers will entangle government in sectarianism, forcing taxpayers to support religious ideas and practices—and religious bigotry—that are anathema to them.

According to the National Center for Educational Statistics[11], 78 percent of private schools have a religious foundation. Minorities represent approximately 22 percent of the students enrolled at all private schools. Additionally nearly 15 percent of private schools have no minority students attending classes. The fact that private schools may discriminate on the basis of income, coupled with the racially skewed income disparities in our society, assures that vouchers will spur school segregation. Nadine Strossen, president of the American Civil Liberties Union penned the following regarding the statewide school voucher program that was signed into law by Florida Governor Jeb Bush:

> ...far from expanding "choice" or "opportunity," as their advocates assert, vouchers instead reduce the educational options and opportunities available to precisely those students and parents who already have the fewest choices, including the poor and minorities. Therefore, vouchers violate

the 14th Amendment equality guarantee, as well as the First Amendment's religious-liberty guarantee, which is why the ACLU opposes them.[12]

Analysis also shows that parents favor schools that have a higher proportion of white students, giving credence to the notion that school choice could lead to increased income and racial segregation.[13]

CHARTERING A NEW COURSE

In the U.S. context, charter schools represent the full embodiment of the concept of self-governing schools within the public school system. Such schools are public in that they receive public funding and are ultimately accountable to the same public authority. What differentiates charter schools is that they are not operated directly by the government. Rather, many of them are established and managed by voluntary associations of parents, educators, citizens, and others who come together with a common vision of education. Some charter schools are sponsoring pre-existing organizations such as community groups, teachers' unions, churches, and even private businesses. Although in some cases regular public schools have converted to charter status, the majority of charter schools have started from scratch. Each school has a charter and is exempt from the need to follow many of the usual rules and procedures imposed on other public schools.[14]

Charter schools, meant to foster competition with traditional public schools, are exempted from following several of the rules of the game. The best analogy is akin to playing Checkers with a five year old. The rules of the game seem to change in favor of the child at every turn. And there is logic behind each deviation from the norm. There is a wise adage that suggests that the difficulty with arguing with a five year old is that soon one starts to sound like a five year old.

What are the rules that are so trivial to the playing field? In Wisconsin, charter schools do not fall under the following statutes:

- Statutes regarding the education of handicapped students

- Guidelines dictating pupil removal from classes

- Controls of the length of the school year

- Mandated programs for gifted and talented students

- Mandated programs for instruction in English

To advocates and critics, charter schools make strong—but contradictory—statements about democracy. To advocates, charter schools represent perhaps the last great American educational hope within the public sector. They are not only an opportunity to secure publicly funded education for students, but also an avenue for parents, teachers, and administrators to exert more direct influence over what is taught and learned. Critics counter that charter schools and educational choice are proof positive that the ideals of the common school have been abandoned.[15]

TELL HER WHAT SHE'S WON, JOHNNY

Will charter schools create an uncommon "commune-ality"? Some critics caution that a renewed and vigorous segregation of the student population could occur, because like-minded parents and educators have the freedom to create schools that cater to a specific, targeted clientele—a type of voluntary segregation that could cluster affluent students, students of color, or English language learners in their own schools. And although charter schools are not exempt from federal civil rights and special education legislation, if their operators and staff choose to market their programs only to a select clientele, they conceivably could avoid specific student populations.[16]

Competition is often associated with athletics. Athletic regulations, however, often equalize competitions. Boxers, for example, are assigned a class. Heavyweights and featherweights cannot be competitive in the same ring. Additionally, it is not a fair fight. Similarly, the promotion of charter versus traditional public schooling is not a fair comparison. When one institution can ignore those rules that have the most fiscal and sociological implications and the other cannot, there is a distinct disadvantage for the more regulated institution.[17]

Charter schools look good on paper. Gathering groups of motivated people for a common purpose creates energy and renewed enthusiasm for education. Commune-ality abounds. However, charter schools may also be perceived as the "wedge that pries open the doorway through which the for-profit sector can enter the growing educational industry."[18]

Many charter schools have their roots in simplicity. Educators, parents, and administrators simply wanted to "do" education differently. Charter schools emerged from passionate belief systems about how children should be educated. Increasingly, however, charter schools are being managed by larger for-profit firms. Charter school laws in at least 12 states allow for management by for-profit firms and as of 1997, 10 percent of the 750 charter schools were run by for-profit ventures, referred to as Education Management Organizations (EMOs).[19] The business community's support for initiatives like charter schools is explicable as blatant self-interest. However, public acceptance of increased private sector involvement depends heavily on the corporate promoted conception that the private sector, because it is rooted in competition, is inherently better than the public sector. And on very hot days, the top folds down, too.

A BOX OF CHOCOLATES

Forrest Gump will be forever credited with teaching us that "life is like a box of chocolates, you never know what you're going to get until you try it." So it is with curriculum, teaching styles, and even educational environments. The perception of "failing American schools" is, in part, based on circular reasoning. It is ludicrous to imagine that because change is sought that the status quo is bad. Parents seek alternative educational environments for a variety of reasons. Advocates of increased privatization would have us believe that the ebb and flow of students from the public to the private sectors is based on a "lack of confidence" in the public schools. I bought a different brand of peanut butter last week. It had the jelly mixed into it and I wanted to try it. Does that means I no longer like the brand that I've been using for the past ten years? Of course not, it simply means that I both wanted to try something new and had the funds available to splurge a bit.

Peanut butter, of course, is a consumable resource. My selection of it has far less impact than the type of school that I select for my child. The point is only this—public school confidence is affected by negative reports of poor public school confidence. Such reports make their claims through inappropriate inference. It is an inference that derails the public's confidence. Which came first—public school decline or the marketed perception of it?

NO BUSINESS LIKE THE KNOW BUSINESS

Education spending represents 10 percent of the United States gross national product, but only two-tenths of one percent of the stock market. This represents a fabulous opportunity for profit-taking to those entrepreneurs the National Education Association labels "edventurists." *The New York Times* predicts that education could be turned into "the next health care."[20] If education is to be reformed according to business rules, business alone will decide how to best benefit from the enormous potential investment opportunity. The prospect of increased privatization of the public education system has launched a series of new businesses, which speaks volumes about the direction that public schools are taking in the market economy. First Marblehead is a private company that offers loans to cash-strapped students. Although these loans are predominantly for postsecondary education, First Marblehead has begun to enter the K–12 market to aid parents at "reasonable" interest rates, who wish to send their children to private schools. This scenario potentially places children in debt beginning from the age of five.[21]

Edventurists and their proponents seek to create a nationwide, market-driven school choice educational system that destroys a perceived monopoly held by public schools. Statistically, the 80 to 88 percent of children who attend public schools appear well above the threshold that the U.S. Justice Department's Anti-Trust Division uses to define a monopoly. The only trouble is, that definition is used in reference to businesses. Merrifield goes on to state that "school principals have neither the profit motive nor the options [to spread successful practices to other places] and concerns [bankruptcy] that characterize the producers in competitive markets."[22]

Gee, a job without a financial bottom line? A career where the hearts and minds of America's children are more important than their pocketbooks?

Assume that the misguided analysis of schools as monopolies has merit. Then, wouldn't it be more profitable for my local library to rent the books? Shouldn't my city's fire and police agencies charge me for any emergency I encounter? Public parks could make a tidy profit if they charged the children to play or the adults to commune with nature. The unilateral tossing away of institutions dedicated to the public good or the creation of fee structures within those institutions creates instability at best and measurable harm at worst.

How do edventurists both provide "value" and make profits? Here are a few of the ways[23]:

• Reduce labor costs, through cuts in employment and union-busting

• Provide fewer student services, such as, transportation, school lunches, intramural athletics, band and orchestra, and extracurricular activities

• Specialize in the education of less costly students—for example, regular K–12 students rather than limited English or special needs students

• Encourage and retain only those students most likely to succeed

• Substitute self-paced computer instruction or videos for regular teaching staff

• Discriminate against kids who need special education

• Charge fees

• Install a cookie-cutter curriculum, geared to testing criteria and a packaged testing system

NOTHING EDVENTURED, NOTHING GAINED

Schools as big business change the bottom line of public education. Mission statements that speak for the children, for their rights, and for their development as global citizens will need to be reconsidered. Bumper stickers that tout "School and Community, Working Together" and "All Children Can Learn" will need to be replaced. I have a few suggestions for those new bumper stickers.

• Making $1.99 an Hour on YOUR Child

• Learn to Pay to Learn

• Students Behind the Bottom Line (SBBL)

• Helping You, Help Us

- The Three R's . . . Real Returns of Revenue

- Nothing Edventured, Nothing Gained

Just as I am dismayed by the notion of commercialism directed at the captive audience of America's youth, I am frightened by the idea of using children for profit. Images of Willy Wonka's "Good Egg/Bad Egg" machine come to mind and the wails of Veronica Salt as she was sent away to the trash compost. In a business that produces any sort of good or service, such a machine is necessary. No one wants to find a foreign substance on their pepperoni pizza. When the bottom line is profit, strict measures must be observed and standardized for sorting the good from the bad.

If the money mongers have their way and an agenda of for-profit education is installed in American schools, what will become of first-grade Jessica who does not learn as fast as the others? Of wheelchair-bound Edron? Of Tamilla and Bobby, who are diagnosed with Down's syndrome? It is critical to understand that even if teachers must keep these students in their classrooms under the umbrella of equalization, a precedent has been set for discrimination and bias. Teachers who are trained and employed to work towards an increased financial bottom line will see their students with dollar signs tattooed on their foreheads. The heart of education will have been traded for thirty pieces of silver and students with the potential of Albert Einstein will be discarded along the way. Anna Freud once said, "Creative minds have always been known to survive any kind of bad training." Let's hope that it's true.

FARE THEE WELL?

Nontraditional educational options such as vouchers, charters, and for-profit privatized business ventures are no longer speculative theories. Evidence of their existence stretches across the United States. So, how have such programs fared?

It would be simple to say that such programs have failed. It would be equally easy to offer that they have succeeded. Strong evidence seems to abound on both sides of the issue and an author need only determine where to make a stand.

It is difficult to take issue with the concepts of parents being provided educational choices. The ability to pursue one's ideals is an integral element of American culture. Spending more to drive a convertible and earning enough to be chauffeured in a stretch limousine are more than the American privilege; they are an American right. Part of the American reality, however, is that some people have always gotten more choices than others. Affluence and social position have impacted most decisions— even the decisions about who is elected into political office. It is narrowminded to think that money alone will provide equalization. Without a convergence of social programs, those living in poverty will continue to have token choices. It is unfair and unethical to tout public education as a political platform or a commentary on parenting. Unfortunately, it is easier to use dollars as Band-Aids for the greater social ills that eclipse many parts of our society.

The presence of such social ills brings to light the American responsibility. Life in a privileged culture demands accountability to a higher standard if that privilege is to survive. It is not enough to wish it better. It is not enough to provide funds. Failing schools are a by-product of failing communities. Failing communities are a by-product of a failing society. No one, especially those immersed in failure, wish it to be that way. Punishments and scorn will not make the situation more tolerable. Competition only makes the playing field visible for what it is.

In *Educational Renaissance*, Marvin Cetron and Margaret Gayle take yet another opportunity to bemoan the state of American education. They speak of the poor outcomes of failing institutions of learning. They relate that "companies have tried a rich variety of ideas to aid our schools."[24] Those companies will ride up on sleek horses and wear white hats for just as long as we in public education allow them to. For-profit agencies will capitalize on the public distrust that politicians, policy makers, and the media offer at every turn. If you've ever had a vacuum cleaner salesman in your living room, you will realize that there will always be those that play on other people's insecurities in the pursuit of financial gain.

It is not time to equalize education. It is time to equalize the partnerships that education makes with the publics that it serves. It is time to stop being grateful for the scraps that fall from the corporate table and it is time to stop being threatened by the unenlightened sanctions of those for whom a vote is more important than a conscience. It is time for educators across America to become the professionals that we are and have always been. It is time to stand up and do what we do best—teach to the heart of each child.

CHAPTER SEVEN

NO ONE IS LEFT BEHIND
THE CHILD

The No Child Left Behind plan implemented by George W. Bush's administration will have long-term and detrimental effects on the American public school system. This chapter examines those effects.

BUILD IT, AND THEY WILL COME

My clothes dryer broke the other day. It was in midcycle with a load of heavy jeans and sweatshirts and it just quit working. I hauled my still-damp clothes out and placed them in a heap on the kitchen counter, wondering what to do. Accountability and standards, I told myself and I rushed to my dryer to explain. At first, I spoke in an even tone, gently making clear that there were quality standards to be met and a certain level of performance that was expected. My dryer refused to cooperate, offering only its full lint trap as an indicator of what could have gone so terribly wrong. Words alone were not enough. I emptied the lint trap and still, nothing. There was no pleasing whir of sound to indicate that all was again as it should be. I began to rant and rave and threaten to withhold all laundry if my dryer wouldn't do as I bade. Still, my words were useless. Desperately, I used my wrenches and cunning to try to fix the dryer. And I was successful! I found and diagnosed the problem and once again had fresh, clean, and dry laundry.

My neighbor down the street wasn't so lucky. She cajoled and tried to bribe her dryer. She held the owner's manual over her dryer's metal exterior, hoping to make it see the error of its ways. She tweaked and prodded and cried and still her laundry lay in a sodden heap. Finally, in spite of living within an extremely tight budget, she called in a specialist. The solution, she was told, was costly and wouldn't come in time to save her current load of laundry. And there was no guarantee that the system simply wouldn't fail again.

It was in this state of confusion and frustration that she arrived on my doorstep, her wet laundry in a needy heap by her side. The best advice she had been given, she said, was to find a dryer that worked. I welcomed her in and together we made her laundry accountable to meet its goal of being useable and dry.

It was easy and rewarding to help her. I even felt a bit smug at my ability to have created a system that someone else wanted and needed. It didn't really matter that I had a better machine to start with or that I had more money to invest in keeping my machine running; it only mattered that I had somehow managed to maintain a system that worked. I was flattered and a little bit arrogant as we tossed in dryer sheets and pressed the "start" button.

Until the doorbell rang again. And again. People started coming from all over the place, neighbors from down the street and strangers from across the city. They all were burdened with cumbersome unfinished business. My dryer began to have to work day and night to keep up with the demand. The windows in my house steamed with the moisture in the air and the sound of the nasal buzz of the machine was never far away. My dryer became overworked, poorly maintained, and underfunded. When I heard the gears grind to a raucous, screaming halt, I knew that there would be no revival of my system. I knew that I would be forced to join the rest of the wrinkled and hapless on a pilgrimage to find a better system somewhere else.

So it is with the educational policies enacted by the Bush administration. Touted as a plan to promote equity and high standards and highlighted as a display of governmental bipartisan support, the plan calls for schools, like clothes dryers, to operate at maximum efficiency. It offers some monies toward the maintenance of those dryers...but only enough to offset the initial fixes. The plan encourages the public to be consumers of their education, seeking better clothes dryers outside of their local neighborhoods if necessary. Strangely, it doesn't address the many problems that are inherent in the vision or the enactment of the plan.

There is an old cartoon that depicts a leather clad Viking standing at the helm of an ancient sailing vessel. The crew is obviously beleaguered and weary. The Viking is wearing a scowl and holding a whip. The caption on the picture reads, "The beatings will continue until morale improves."

Thus it seems to be with the morale of public education. The No Child Left Behind policy states that if schools are to be held to high standards, they must have the freedom to meet those standards. The freedom to do as commanded is an oxymoron. It is not so much an invitation to excel as an acknowledgement that there will be failure. In fact, the plan further states, . . . "students that fail to make sufficient progress should receive special assistance. Students should not be forced to attend persistently failing schools and must, at some point, be freed to attend adequate schools. Under this plan, disadvantaged students will not be required to sacrifice their education and future for the sake of preserving the status quo."[1]

Consider the words *adequate, disadvantaged, sacrifice,* and *status quo.* Nowhere are there good schools. Nowhere are there unmotivated and apathetic students. Like the wet laundry in the analogy, students under the President's plan are perceived to be passive and powerless recipients of the educational process. The students in the President's vision are innately resilient and eager to learn. A low-quality curriculum and a lack of professionalism on behalf of their teachers consistently thwart their efforts. They are forced to become educational nomads in search of schools that will provide the quality that has been out-of-reach for them for so long.

There is not a school in our nation that wants its students to maintain a status quo of ignorance, poverty, or disillusionment.

It defies common sense to imagine that teachers head to disadvantaged schools each day to make no difference. Painting a picture of classrooms filled with disappointed eager learners and oppressive, ignorant, apathetic teachers does little to assuage the wounds already inflicted on education by a misinformed public.

In a comprehensive plan that eerily resembles a corporate manifesto, there is a written expectation of yearly progress for disadvantaged youth, corrective action for low-functioning schools, fiscal rewards for schools with satisfactory test scores, and monetary and job-related consequences for failure. Perhaps if the product were pizza, these mandates would be realistic. Even then, however, one should consider the work of Dr. W. Edward Deming, a leader in total quality management (TQM). Author John Bonstingl has applied Deming's Fourteen Points of TQM to the public school setting and has reached the following conclusions:

• Maximization of test scores and assessment symbols is less important than the progress inherent in continuous learning.

• Cynical application of the new philosophy, with the sole intent of improving district-wide test scores, destroys the interpersonal trust essential to success.

• **Reliance on tests as the major means of assessment of student production is inherently wasteful** and often neither reliable nor authentic. (emphasis added)

• Learning is best shown through student performance in applying information and skills to real life challenges.

• **Fear is counterproductive in schools.** It is destructive of the school culture and everything good that is intended to take place within it. (emphasis added)

• When educational goals are not met, [one should] fix the system instead of fixing blame on individuals.

• When grades [and subsequently test scores] becomes the bottom line product, short-term gains replace student investment in long-term learning.

• **Leading is helping, not threatening or punishing.** (emphasis added)[2]

THE CARROT OR THE STICK?

As part of their public school improvement efforts, the Bush administration put into place a consolidation of the Eisenhower Professional Development funds and the monies available for the Class Size Reduction program. The assumption was made that there would be more flexibility available for teacher training and improvement with the combined funds. It is a good idea. Ongoing continuing education opportunities are vital to the professionalism of teachers. But teacher education comes at a cost. First, it generally means time out of the classroom. With the substitute teacher crisis that public schools currently face, allowing teachers time away from school to do professional development is an impossibility for many districts. Secondly, true quality reform efforts are not maintainable from "shot in the arm" inservices or generalized trainings that provide basic information only. Without a prescriptive means for follow-through, most new programs, even good ones, are lost to the other demands on a teacher's time. Finally, and most seriously, the plan calls for "disclosing to parents information about the quality of their child's teacher, as defined by the state." Will quality mean adequate test scores within a classroom? If so, there will be an even greater strain on those teachers who consistently receive the disenfranchised and special education students in their classrooms because they are "good" with them. Will quality mean good student attendance? Newspaper recognition? A reduction in incidents of violence? An increase in English-speaking abilities among students? Notable acts of character from children in a particular class? Shouldn't quality, which is at best a subjective adjective in the pen of the beholder, be as differentiated among teachers as the instructional abilities we expect of these teachers? Efforts to quantify the spirit of educators will result in a cookie-cutter curriculum delivered by a uniform staff of gingerbread teachers. And that's the way the cookie crumbles.

I BEFORE E, EXCEPT AFTER C

My fifth-grade son, who is not a natural speller, had to learn seventeen of the states for his last spelling test. He also had to know their locations and postal abbreviations. The abbreviations and locations were mastered readily and then the questions started. "But Mom, why does Vermont have an 'er' and Virginia have an 'ir' and why does Georgia start with a 'G' and Jersey start with a 'J'?" I didn't have an answer, save for the fact that the English language has derived from the melting pot that is the American heritage. Imagine how it must be for students from another culture who are suddenly immersed in the English language in their schools. There is a vast amount for them to learn. The No Child Left Behind plan attempts to address this issue. The reasons for the concern on behalf of the federal government are astounding. The policy states, "Research has shown that English language learners, when compared to their English-fluent peers, tend to receive lower grades and often score below the average on standardized math and reading assessments." First of all, it is incredible that this finding comes as a surprise to anyone. If we sent American students to Mexico and gave them standardized tests in Spanish, would they not be at a significant disadvantage? Secondly, it is implausible to think that increased, higher-stakes testing can improve this condition. One begins to wonder if we want students to learn the English language or only the language as it applies to test taking.

Advocates of the standardized testing process might argue that testing students on the concepts taught in their native language is the answer. Realistically, however, this solution also has some serious drawbacks. Many foreign-born students arrive at American schools not only not conversant in English, but functionally illiterate in their native languages as well. It was extremely frustrating as a principal to experience communication with families only when a verbal translator was available. Families could not read any of the information required to enroll their children in school and could not keep advised of their children's progress *even when communiqués were sent in their native language.*

Many immigrant children have undergone serious hardships in their migration to the United States. Not only do they have a lack of early learning experiences, they have little school readiness and often must be taught basic social skills (cultural norms) while being taught the English language. Expecting public schools to increase English fluency is appropriate. Providing and removing funds based on the perceived success of that teaching is shortsighted. There are simply too many unforeseen loopholes. At a minimum, it should be realized that students with Limited English Proficiency tend to have higher rates of transition to other geographic areas than their peers. In addition, there are cultural mores present in families that may directly inhibit school success. It must be remembered that parents, too, may just be in the early stages of learning the English language and becoming familiar with the often subtle cultural norms in the United States.

NO INTEREST UNTIL 2005

"Systems are often resistant to change—no matter how good the intentions of those who lead them. Competition can be the stimulus a bureaucracy needs in order to change.... Parents, armed with data, are the best forces of accountability in education, and parents, armed with options and choice, can assure that their children get the best, most effective education possible."[3]

Perhaps more than any other statement in the No Child Left Behind policy, this statement is demoralizing and detrimental to the hard work that is happening each day in America's classrooms. People take up arms when their security is threatened. In the Bush plan, parents are presumed to be virtual Don Quixotes, rescuing their victimized learners from the cruel hands of low-quality professionals and failing, dangerous schools. Parents are encouraged to take an active role in slaying the impersonal institutions that have harbored ill will towards their child. Providing a competitive educational market is seen as a key factor in delivering increasingly effective curriculum to students. Viewed with corporate vision, there is a tacit understanding that when the producers of a service or product must vie for customers, consumers will get better products at lower prices with more efficient delivery and better service. However, even in a model of pure consumerism, this is not the case. Products can be made more eye-catching. They can be streamlined. They can be better packaged and delivered more rapidly. They can even be made more cost effective. However, none of these factors is an indicator of their quality . . . only of their popularity.

SEE YOUR DEALER FOR DETAILS

Remember those student council elections from your high school days? How often did the best candidate get elected to the executive board? How often did the election results simply boil down to a popularity contest? Movies are made about the triumph of the "have-nots" over the "haves." Movies are made because it is the unexpected ideal and not the status quo. Forcing competition between schools will procure the same slanted and unfair results. Schools with good athletic programs will attract students first, those with a quality drama and music program will attract still others, and as with real estate, there is always the matter of location, location, location. Given a choice between attending the school with the new auditorium and the natatorium and health center, how many parents will choose the school across town that is alleged to have a more well-developed curriculum? Decisions, even major life decisions, are not guided merely on intellect. Aesthetics, emotion, and practicality play important roles in the decision-making process. A measurable, standardized, test-worthy curriculum is not going to make a public school located on the "wrong side of the tracks" attractive enough to students out of wealthier, safer neighborhoods. In the case of public education, competition will not spur improvement; it will increase enrollments at affluent schools and heighten tension for those students left behind.

The negative impacts of educational competition will not end with an increase in underachieving inner-city schools. As with the star-bellied sneeches of Suess lore, soon there will be a glut on the market that will result in pandemonium and chaos for children. Schools that garner public favor will not be able to keep up with demand, especially when they start receiving high numbers of troubled students from neighboring schools. Like other societal trends, education will begin to reflect an odd combination of whimsy and rhetoric and schools will begin to segregate themselves unwittingly. A right-wing conservative fundamentalist? PS 21 has the program for you. A left-wing free thinker? PS 34 will be more to your liking. Undecided? Try PS 53. For a short time only, they are giving a free textbook with every enrollment to qualified applicants. See dealer for details.

ARE YOU A GOOD WITCH
OR A BAD WITCH?

"... This title ensures that parents know whether their child attends a safe school and frees students from those that are dangerous."[4]

I know my son's teachers. All of them. I know where his classroom is, what he is currently studying, who his friends are, and what the cafeteria serves for lunch each day. I know how safe he feels, emotionally and physically, in his classroom. I know which students he doesn't like to sit near because they are disruptive or are bullies. I know these things because it is my job as a responsible parent to know them. I don't know them because of a mandate that schools communicate with parents.

Schools have always communicated with parents. Overtly, schools send newsletters, permission slips, handbooks, pamphlets, and the literature of a thousand trees home each year. Covertly, our children bring us messages about the work and the play that goes on in their world for eight or more hours each day. Responsible parents actively listen to their children, inquire about their classrooms, and keep tabs on their learning. A mandate that schools report their "safety" to parents using state-defined standards does little to enhance the efforts of already responsible parents; instead, it reflects the negativism that the federal government is harboring towards American's public schools.

How does a school become "persistently dangerous"? The most frequent aims of student violence in schools are retribution for a perceived wrong, seeking to make another student desist from a course of action, self-defense, and promotion of one's image or reputation.[5]

Adapting a curriculum that focuses on civic values and conflict resolution is only one of the steps recommended by the Task Force on School Violence.[6] This report also calls for tougher weapon laws, improvement in juvenile codes, strong partnerships between community social work agencies and schools, more early education, increased partnerships between schools and law enforcement agencies, and more funding for Student Assistance Programs and alternative schools.

School safety is not an issue exclusively owned by America's public schools. Will allowing students to migrate to schools deemed "safe" make the media more responsible? Parents more involved? Gangs less prevalent? And what if the parents of the students who participate in acts of violence want their child to have the option of a safer school environment? Is it likely that being in a classroom across town will make a bully see the error of his ways?

We live in a country in which segregation is viewed as a negative phenomenon. Yet, we also live in a culture where discrimination is evident in subtle and not-so-subtle ways. School systems that espouse "zero tolerance" as is mandated by the President's plan, need to be able to enforce that policy. However, tighter controls have never been the sole motivation behind behavioral change. There will be students that test the system. Some of them will be students that the school system is able to expel, although this causes a whole new set of societal problems. Others, will be special education students who the District must educate differently or elsewhere, because expulsion would be in conflict with their exceptional needs. Where will these students go? Separate facilities? Separate but equal? It is not likely.

Schools are a microcosm of society. The intent of a school is to be safe, healthy, and productive. A multitude of societal factors (discussed in Chapter Four) break down that intent. The No Child Left Behind plan seems to contradict itself. Schools will get funding for providing a safe and drug-free environment for students to become good test takers. The picture is painted of students held captive by schools that do not reflect these conditions. These students, it is purported, need to be "freed" from the dangerous conditions of their educational system. So far, so good. It seems that the "good guys" are going to be given increased monies to welcome more "good guys" to their fold. But what about the students left behind?

I've talked with many parents who did not know their child's teacher. I met some parents for the first time at their child's eighth-grade graduation. Still others, I never met at all. There are many factors behind parental apathy. Under the Bush plan, that apathy will extend itself to irresponsibility. Unfortunately, the victims of that irresponsibility will be the children who are left behind in underfunded, underachieving schools.

This is where the Bush plan seems to contradict itself. The plan calls for achievement without really giving schools in poverty a fighting chance. The velvet atop the iron fist does little to assuage the blow that the federal government is dealing inner-city schools. Students with responsible parents will leave for more affluent options, leaving behind the nonperformers and the children whose parents do not wish to make school choices. Predictably, the pool of students remaining at schools-in-need will do poorly on standardized tests and even more funding will be lost.

In fact, it is my prediction that such schools will become the "alternative schools" of the future, meant to house the lowest common denominators in all classrooms. It will be easier for districts to have one or two underachieving schools filled with poor test takers than it will be to have those students spread out among schools. In the pizza factory mentioned in the introduction to this book, unwanted product was turned into dog food. What does America plan to do with the students who can't or won't receive an assembly line education?

FORCED ELECTIVES

When I first became a middle school principal, the students had several elective choices within their school day. They were able to take courses that appealed to their imaginations, interests, and creativity. However, as the pressure of meeting a host of educational standards increased, those electives dwindled down to a set of electives so narrow that they became "forced." That is, they were really requirements with little room for flexibility.

Title VII of the No Child Left Behind plan[7] states that "school districts will be granted unprecedented flexibility by this proposal in how they spend federal education funds. Accountability for student results is expected in return. States and schools that make significant progress will be honored with rewards. The Secretary of Education will be authorized to withhold administrative funds from states that fail to make adequate progress."

When there is intense and direct pressure to perform well on standardized tests, there is not flexibility. When a school knows that its "report card" will be on display each year, and that the crux of that report card will be standardized test performance, there is no flexibility. There is not even any comfort in the fact that the test scores of a school will be reflected based on factors such as poverty, English proficiency, and numbers of students with disabilities. There is not any comfort because both the media and the American people have proven themselves to be "bottom liners" over and over again. No one wants to read the small print, and the large print of the headlines is sure to be the sole testimony of most public schools.

In *Punished By Rewards,* Alfie Kohn says, "The aggressive attempt to 'make' children do something—and even more absurd to 'make' them care about what they were made to do—is a recipe for failure."[8]

I am getting a picture in my mind of the high-achieving school of the twenty-first century. There will be smiling politicians shaking hands with beaming school administrators. They will be surrounded by the tomes of curricular standards that school staffs have created and recreated over the past five years. Test results will be emblazoned on a large colorful banner over their heads. In the background, there will be stacks of test preparation materials, towers of manuals, scores of answer sheets, and a sea of No. 2 pencils. All of that will be there in sharp focus. There will be only one thing missing. There will be no child left behind them.

NOTES

Chapter One

1. Condition of Education 1999, National Center for Educational Statistics, Office of Educational Research and Improvement, U.S. Department of Education, Washington, DC. Available online at <http://nces.ed.gov/pubs99/condition99/>.

2. National Education Goals Panel. 1991. "The National Education Goals Report: Building a Nation of Learners." Washington, DC, Author.

3. Information available at <www.mcrel.org/products/standards/fallrise.pdf>. p. 3.

4. Information available at <www.kidsource.com>.

5. Kohn, Alfie. 1999. *The Schools Our Kids Deserve: Moving Beyond Traditional Classrooms and Tougher Standards.* Boston: Houghton Mifflin.

6. Benson, John. 2000. "Standards of the Heart," *School News* 55(8): 20–23.

7. McQuillan, Jeff. 1998. *The Literacy Crisis: False Claims, Real Solutions.* Cambridge, MA: Heinemann Publishing.

8. Information available at <www.frac.org/html/hunger_in_the_us/hunger_index.html>.

9. A Status Report on Hunger and Homelessness in America's Cities: 1997, U.S. Conference of Mayors, December 1997.

10. Palmer, Julian, ed. 1999. "Young Children in Poverty: A Statistical Update." National Center for Children in Poverty. The Joseph Mailman School of Public Health, Columbia University.

11. U.S. Census Bureau. March 2002. *Child Poverty Fact Sheet.* Information available at <www.census.gov>.

12. Kids Count 2000, prepared by the Annie E. Casey Foundation, Baltimore, MD. Information available at <www.aecf.org>.

13. Kipling, Rudyard. 2000. *The Jungle Book.* New York: Dover Publications.

Chapter Two

1. Bonstingl, John. 1992. *Schools of Quality: An Introduction to Total Quality Management in Education.* Alexandria, VA: Association for Supervision and Curriculum Development, pp. 77–82.

2. U.S. Census Bureau 2000. *U.S. Census Quick Facts, 2000.* Information available at <www.census.gov>.

3. Salter, Tom. 2001. "Looking for Love in All the Wrong Places." *School News* (March): 24–25.

4. Molnar, Alex. 1996. *Giving Kids the Business: The Commercialization of America's Schools.* Boulder, CO: Westview Press.

5. Giroux, Henry. 1999. "Corporate Culture and the Attack on Higher Education and Public Schooling." *Phi Delta Kappan International Fastback 442.*

6. Wechsler, Pat. 1997. "This Lesson Brought to You By . . ." *Business Week* (June 30): 69.

7. Molnar, Alex. See note 4.

8. Molnar, Alex. See note 4.

9. *A Nation at Risk.* 1983. National Commission on Excellence in Education. Washington, DC: The Commission.

10. Breuer, Tom. 2001. "Dumbing Down?" *The Scene* 8(8): 7.

Chapter Three

1. Beane, James. 2001. Educational Standards. Panel discussion at the National Middle School Association Conference, November 1–3, Washington. DC.

2. Sacks, Peter. 2000. "Predictable Losers in Testing Schemes." *School Administrator.* (December): online edition. Information available at <http://www.aasa.org/publications/sa/2000_12/s>.

3. McEwen, C., Thomas Dickinson, and Doris Jenkins. 2000. *America's Middle Schools in the 21st Century: Status and Progress.* Westerville, OH: National Middle School Association Publications.

4. Palmer, Parker. 1998. *The Courage to Teach.* San Francisco, CA: Jossey-Bass Publishing.

5. Fiedler, Elizabeth, Elizabeth Foster, and Shirley Schwartz. *The Urban Teacher Challenge Report, 2000.* Made possible by the Council of Great City Schools and Recruiting New Teachers, Inc. Information available at <www.cgcs.org> and <www.rnt.org>.

6. Reich, Robert. 2001. "Standards for What?" *Education Week.* 20(41).

Chapter Four

1. Marzano, Robert and Debra Pickering. 1992. *Dimensions of Learning, Teacher's Manual,* 2nd ed. Alexandria, VA: Association for Supervision and Curriculum Development.

2. Gibbs, Jeanne. 1978. *TRIBES: A Process for Peer Involvement.* Oakland, CA: Center Source Publications.

3. Toppo, Greg. 2001. "Teachers Get Homicide Insurance Offer," abcnews.com, Associated Press.

4. "In America...Facts on Youth, Violence, and Crime." February 2002. Information available at <www.edfactioncouncil.org/americayvc.htm>.

5. "Fact Sheet: Children, Education, and the War on Drugs." 2001. Drug Policy Alliance: Office of National Affairs,

Washington, DC. Information available at <www.drugpolicy.
org/action/fact_children_print.html>.

6. Information available at <www.anotherperspective.org/
advoc297.html>.

7. Nissen, Beth. 2000. "Teachers Say Pay Us More Money
and Respect," *CNN.com* (May) online edition. Information
available at <http://www.cnn.com/2000/US/05/08/teacher.
report/>.

8. Information available at <www.aflcio.org/women/wwfacts.
htm>.

9. Saluter, Arlene. 1994. *Marital Status and Living Arrange-
ments: March 1994.* U.S. Bureau of the Census, March
1996. Information also available at <www.divorcereform.org/
rates.html>.

10. "What Teachers Should Know about the NEA." Released by the Alexis de Tocqueville Institution in *School
Reform News.* Online edition. Information available at
<www.heartland.org/education/sep97/nea.htm>.

11. *Columbia University Record.* 1995. 20(17), February 17.
Information available at <www.columbia.edu/cu/record/
record2017.31.html>.

12. White House Education Press Releases and Statements,
August 21, 2000. Information available at <www.ed.gov/
PressReleases/08-2000/wh-0821.html>.

13. Snyder, T. and C. Hoffman. 1999. *Digest of Education Statistics, 1999—Executive Summary,* U.S. Department of Education, National Center for Education Statistics, Washington,
DC Government printing office.

14. Gray, Ellen. 1987. "Latchkey Children," *ERIC Clearinghouse
for Elementary and Early Childhood Education.* Urbana, IL. ID
ED 290575.

15. "Homeless Children." 1999. *America Magazine.* (November 13) online edition. Information available at <www.
findarticles.com>.

16. Anderson, Amy, Rick Evans, Rich Kozak, and Blair Peterson.
1997. "At Issue: Improving the Perception of Public

Education." *On the Horizon.* Online edition. Chapel Hill, NC: University of North Carolina. Information available at <http://horizon.unc.edu/projects/issues/>.

Chapter Five

1. Snyder, T. and C. Hoffman. 1999. *Digest of Education Statistics, 1999—Executive Summary,* U.S. Department of Education, National Center for Education Statistics, Washington, DC. Government printing office.

2. National Institute on Disability and Rehabilitation Research. Information available at <www.infouse.com/disabilitydata/womendisability_2_3.html>.

3. Information available at <http://www.brainnet.wa.gov/bnprime.html>.

4. Health Information Services, Inc. "One-Third of U.S. Teens Feel Stressed Every Day." October 27, 1999. Reuters Health.

5. Johnson, David and Mark Lino. 2000. "Teenagers: Employment and Contributions to Family Spending." *Monthly Labor Review.* (September): 15–25.

6. Grummon, David. 2000. "The Road to Leadership: Moving Youth from Apathy to Awareness to Responsibility." *Community Links* 12(3). Information available at <www.communitypolicing.org/publications/comlinks/cl_n12/c12_grumm.htm>.

7. Brown, B. V. and Emig, C. 1999. Who Are America's Disconnected Youth? In *America's Disconnected Youth: Toward a Preventive Strategy.* Doug Besharov and Karen Gardiner, eds. Washington, DC: Child Welfare League of America.

8. Gardner, Howard. 1983. *Frames of Mind: The Theory of Multiple Intelligences.* New York: Basic Press.

9. Caine, Renate and Geoffrey Caine. 1997. "Mind Brain Learning Principles." *21st Century Learning Initiative.* Information available at <www.21learn.org>.

10. Perrone, Victor. 1991. "On Standardized Testing." *ERIC Clearinghouse for Elementary and Early Childhood Education.* Urbana, IL.

11. Perrone, Victor. 1976. Position paper on Standardized Testing and Evaluation. Association for Childhood Education and National Association of Elementary Schools Principals Conference. *Childhood Education.* 53: 9–16.

12. *A Nation at Risk.* 1983. National Commission on Excellence in Education. Washington, DC: The Commission.

13. Perrone, Victor. 1976. Position paper on Standardized Testing and Evaluation. Association for Childhood Education and National Association of Elementary Schools Principals Conference. *Childhood Education.* 53: 9–16.

14. "Your Baby's Brainpower." 1996. *Working Mother.*

15. Information available at <www.fairtest.org/arn/University%20Faculty%20Associationoppose.html>.

16. Houston, Paul. 2000. "A Stake Through the Heart of High Stakes Tests." *School Administrator.* (December): online edition. Information available at <http://www.aasa.org/publications/sa/2000_12/s>.

17. Morse, Jodie. 2002. "Test Drive." *Time.com* 159(5). Information available at <www.time.com/time/magazine/printout/0,8816,197647,00.html>.

18. Sandbaum, Jessica. 2001. "Companies Cash In on Testing Trend." *Education Week.* (March 14), 20(26): 1, 26, 28.

Chapter Six

1. "Who Cares about Public Education?" 2001. *UE News.* (March): online edition. Information available at <www.ranknfile-ue.org/uen_pubed.html>.

2. Merrifield, John. 2000. "The School Choice Choices." *Independent Review* 5(2): 189.

3. Goldhaber, Dan. 1997. "School Choice as Education Reform." *Phi Delta Kappan.* October: 143–47.

4. Condition of Education 1996, National Center for Educational Statistics, Office of Educational Research and Improvement, U.S. Department of Education, Washington, DC. Available online at <http://nces.ed.gov/pubs96/condition96/>.

5. Goldhaber, Dan. See note 3.

6. "Bush Still Pushing Vouchers." February 4, 2002, aolnews.com, Associated Press.

7. *UE News,* See note 1.

8. Goldhaber, Dan. See note 3.

9. Condition of Education, 1996. See note 4.

10. Kaminer, Wendy. 1997. "The Hidden Agenda of School Vouchers." *Speakout.com* (November 13, 1997). Information available at <www.speakout.com>.

11. U.S. Department of Education, National Center for Educational Statistics, Private School Survey, 1999–2000.

12. Strossen, Nadine. 1999. "Florida's A+ Plan for School Vouchers Deserves an F." *Speakout.com* (July 22, 1999). Information available at <www.speakout.com>.

13. Goldhaber, Dan. See note 3.

14. Ladd, Helen. 2000. "Market Based Reforms in Urban Education." Paper prepared for the Urban Seminar on *Creating Change in Urban Public Education* organized by William Julius Wilson in cooperation with Robert Wood Johnson Foundation, December 7–8, Cambridge, MA.

15. Ostermeyer, Michael. 2001. "Charter School Freedoms Serve Policy Aims." *Wisconsin Charter Schools Newsletter.* (Winter).

16. Lockwood, Anne. 2002. "Four Views of Charter Schools." *New Leaders for Tomorrow's Schools.* North Central Regional Educational Laboratory. Information available at <www.ncrel.org/cscd/pubs/lead42/42four.htm>.

17. Lockwood, Anne. See note 16.

18. Shaker, Erika. Accessed 2001. "Little Red Schoolhouse, LTD? Charter Schools Expedite Privatization of Education." *The CCPA Education Monitor.* Information available at <www.policyalternatives.ca/publications/edumon/article13.html>.

19. Ladd, Helen. See note 14.

20. *UE News.* See note 1.

21. Shaker, Erica. See note 18.

22. Merrifield, John. See note 2.

23. *UE News.* See note 1.

24. Cetron, Marvin and Margaret Gayle. *Educational Renaissance.* New York: St. Martin's Press.

Chapter Seven

1. "No Child Left Behind" (NCLB). 2002. Department of Education – United States of America. Information available at <www.ed.gov/inits/nclb/part1.html>.

2. Bonstingl, John. 1992. *Schools of Quality: An Introduction to Total Quality Management in Education.* Alexandria, VA: Association for Supervision and Curriculum Development: 77–82.

3. NCLB. See note 1.

4. NCLB. See note 1.

5. Lockwood, Daniel. 1997. "Violence Among Middle and High School Students: Analysis and Implications for Prevention." U.S. Department of Justice: National Institute of Justice Research Brief. (October).

6. Easely, Mike, Bob Etheridge, and Thurman Hampton. 1993. Task Force on School Violence. Prepared for Governor James B. Hunt, Jr. North Carolina.

7. NCLB. See note 1.

8. Kohn, Alfie. 1993. *Punished by Rewards: The Trouble with Gold Stars, Incentive Plans, A's, Praise, and Other Bribes.* Boston: Houghton Mifflin.

BIBLIOGRAPHY

Benson, John. 2000. "Standards of the Heart," *School News.* 55(8): 20–23.

Berliner, D. C. and Biddle, B. J. 1995. *The Manufactured Crisis: Myths, Fraud, and the Attack on America's Public Schools.* Reading, MA: Addison-Wesley.

Bonstingl, John. 1992. *Schools of Quality: An Introduction to Total Quality Management in Education.* Alexandria, VA: Association for Supervision and Curriculum Development.

Bracey, G. W. 1991. "Why Can't They Be Like We Were?" *Phi Delta Kappan* 73: 104–17.

Bracey, G. W. 1997. "The Seventh Bracey Report on the Condition of Public Education." *Phi Delta Kappan* 79: 120–36.

Breuer, Tom. 2001. "Dumbing Down?" *The Scene* 8(8): 7.

Brown, B. V. and Emig, C. 1999. Who are America's disconnected youth? In *America's Disconnected Youth: Toward a Preventive Strategy.* Doug Besharov and Karen Gardiner, eds. Washington, DC: Child Welfare League of America.

Bruner, J. 1996. *The Culture of Education.* Cambridge, MA: Harvard University Press.

Caine, Renate and Geoffrey Caine. 1991. *Making Connections: Teaching and the Human Brain.* Alexandria, VA: Association for Supervision and Curriculum Development.

Cetron, Martin and Margaret Gayle. 1991. *Educational Renaissance.* New York: St. Martin's Press.

Chubb, J. E. and Moe, T. M. 1990. *Politics, Markets, and America's Schools.* Washington, DC: The Brookings Institution.

Condition of Education 1999. National Center for Educational Statistics, Office of Educational Research and Improvement, U.S. Department of Education, Washington, DC.

Darling-Hammond, L. 1997. *The Right to Learn: A Blueprint for Creating Schools That Work.* San Francisco: Jossey-Bass.

Davis, Stan, and Jim Botkin. 1994. *The Monster Under the Bed.* New York: Simon & Schuster.

Deming, W. E. 1986. *Out of the Crisis.* Cambridge, MA: Massachusetts Institute of Technology.

Gardner, Howard. 1983. *Frames of Mind: The Theory of Multiple Intelligences.* New York: Basic Press.

Gibbs, Jeanne. 1978. *TRIBES: A Process for Peer Involvement.* Oakland, CA: Center Source Publications.

Giroux, H., and Purpel, D., eds. 1983. *The Hidden Curriculum and Moral Education.* Berkely, CA: McCutchan Publishing.

Gross, Martin. 1999. *The Conspiracy of Ignorance: The Failure of American Public Schools.* New York: HarperCollins.

Hershberg, T. 1997. "Explaining Standards: A 12-point Talking Paper." [Commentary]. *Education Week,* December: 33–35.

Houston, Paul. 2000. "A Stake Through the Heart of High Stakes Tests." *School Administrator.* (December).

Johnson, David and Mark Lino. 2000. "Teenagers: Employment and Contributions to Family Spending." *Monthly Labor Review.* (September): 15–25.

Kohn, Alfie. 1992. *No Contest: The Case Against Competition.* rev. ed. Boston: Houghton Mifflin.

Kohn, Alfie. 1993. *Punished by Rewards: The Trouble with Gold Stars, Incentive Plans, A's, Praise, and Other Bribes.* Boston: Houghton Mifflin.

Kohn, Alfie.1999. *The Schools Our Kids Deserve: Moving Beyond Traditional Classrooms and Tougher Standards.* Boston: Houghton Mifflin.

Kozol, Jonathan. 1992. *Savage Inequalities.* New York: Harper Perennial.

Ladd, Helen. 2000. "Market Based Reforms in Urban Education." Paper prepared for the Urban Seminar on *Creating Change in Urban Public Education* organized by William Julius Wilson in cooperation with Robert Wood Johnson Foundation, December 7–8, Cambridge, MA.

Lieberman, Myron. 1993. *Public Education: An Autopsy.* Cambridge, MA: Harvard University Press.

MacLeod, Jay. 1995. *Ain't No Makin' It: Aspirations & Attainment in a Low-Income Neighborhood.* Boulder, CO: Westview Press.

Marzano, Robert J. 1992. *A Different Kind of Classroom: Teaching with Dimensions of Learning.* Alexandria, VA: Association for Supervision and Curriculum Development.

Marzano, Robert and Debra Pickering. 1992. *Dimensions of Learning, Teacher's Manual,* 2nd ed. Alexandria, VA: Association for Supervision and Curriculum Development.

McEwen, Kenneth, Thomas Dickinson, and Doris Jenkins. 2000. *America's Middle Schools in the 21st Century: Status and Progress.* Westerville, OH: National Middle School Association Publications.

McQuillan, Jeff. 1998. *The Literacy Crisis: False Claims, Real Solutions.* Cambridge, MA: Heinemann Publishing.

Meier, Deborah. 2000. *Will Standards Save Public Education?* Boston: Beacon.

Merrifield, John. 2000. "The School Choice Choices." *Independent Review* 5(2): 189.

Molnar, Alex. 1996. *Giving Kids the Business: The Commercialization of America's Schools.* Boulder, CO: Westview Press.

A Nation at Risk. 1983. National Commission on Excellence in Education. Washington, DC: The Commission.

National Education Goals Panel. 1991. "The National Education Goals Report: Building a Nation of Learners." Washington DC, Author.

"No Child Left Behind" (NCLB). 2002. Department of Education – United States of America. Information available at <www.ed.gov/inits/nclb/part1.html>.

Palmer, Parker. 1998. *The Courage to Teach*. San Francisco, CA: Jossey-Bass Publishing.

Ravitch, Diane. 2000. *Left Back: A Century of Failed School Reforms*. NY: Simon & Schuster.

Reich, Robert. 2001. "Standards for What?" *Education Week*. 20(41).

Salter, Tom. 2001. "Looking for Love in All the Wrong Places." *School News*. March: 24–25.

Schmoker, M., and Robert Marzano. 1999. Realizing the Promise of Standards-Based Education. *Educational Leadership* 56(6): 17–21.

Snyder, T. and C. Hoffman. 1999. *Digest of Education Statistics, 1999—Executive Summary*, U.S. Department of Education, National Center for Education Statistics, Washington, DC. Government printing office.

Tyack, David and Larry Cuban. 1995. *Tinkering Toward Utopia: A Century of Public School Reform*. Cambridge, MA: Harvard University Press.

Wechsler, Pat. 1997. "This Lesson Brought to You By . . ." *Business Week* June 30: 69.